FOOD, FARMER, AND COMMUNITY

FOOD, FARMER, AND COMMUNITY

AGRICULTURE AND THE RECONSTRUCTION OF THE WORLD

COMPILED BY WINNONA MERRITT
FOREWORD BY PAUL HANLEY

BAHÁ'Í
PUBLISHING

WILMETTE, ILLINOIS

Bahá'í Publishing
401 Greenleaf Avenue, Wilmette, Illinois 60091

25   24   23   22   4   3   2   1

Library of Congress Control Number: 2021059072
ISBN 978-1-61851-211-6

Cover and book design by Patrick Falso

CONTENTS

FOREWORD

Given that the Bahá'í Faith is the first world religion to emerge in the industrial era, it is perhaps surprising that the discourse of its Central Figures contains so many references to agriculture—many more than in any past revelation. Yet, any serious reading of our reality shows that agricultural systems will always be central to the function of civilization.

In this welcome compilation of quotations from the sacred Bahá'í writings and the letters and statements of Shoghi Effendi and various Bahá'í institutions and agencies, we have at hand a wide-ranging contribution to the discourse on agriculture, from foundational spiritual concepts to practical ideas for the transformation of food systems.

It should be noted that Bahá'u'lláh and 'Abdu'l-Bahá were themselves directly engaged in agriculture at various stages in their lives. Bahá'u'lláh was involved in the management of His family estates prior to His imprisonment and exile from His native Iran. Even as a child, 'Abdu'l-Bahá accompanied His Father in this work, and later He established a community that became a model agricultural village in Jordan—one that offers many lessons for contemporary social, economic, and environmental development activities in rural areas.

The Bahá'í Revelation aims at nothing less than the transformation of the world's order, and agriculture is identified as central to the transformative process. In the Tablet of the World, Bahá'u'lláh outlines concepts that are "conducive to the advancement of mankind and the reconstruction of the world." Specifically, He states that agriculture is foremost among the fundamental principles for the administration of human affairs.

Following from this overarching theme, the quotations gathered here cover a broad range of topics that address the role of agriculture in the reconstruction of world order: the role played by individuals, communities, and institutions; the specific role of women and youth; and the importance of consultation and public discourse in grassroots development processes. The quotations then address a profound understanding of the natural order, from religious and scientific perspectives, including principles around food and health. The writings describe principles of a "divine economy," as well as specific measures that help to build both spiritual and material foundations for the renewal of civilization. Finally, the theme of "divine assistance" in resolving problems impacting farmers and other actors in food systems is addressed.

We owe a debt of gratitude to the compiler of this volume, Winnona Merritt, for her longstanding efforts to assemble the precious writings that provide foundations for our ongoing exploration of the future of agriculture in the emerging World Order of Bahá'u'lláh.

Paul Hanley
June 2021

NOTE TO THE READER

The scripture of the Bahá'í Faith is comprised of the writings of the Faith's Prophet-Founder Bahá'u'lláh (1817–92); His forerunner and Prophet-Herald, the Báb (1819–50); and His son and appointed successor 'Abdu'l-Bahá (1844–1921). Their writings, along with those of Shoghi Effendi (the appointed successor of 'Abdu'l-Bahá, and the Guardian of the Bahá'í Faith from 1921 until his passing in 1957) and the Universal House of Justice, are considered authoritative by Bahá'ís. Established in 1963, the Universal House of Justice is the elected international governing body of the Bahá'í global community and an institution ordained in the writings of Bahá'u'lláh. Selections from other sources, such as those of international agencies of the Faith, while not authoritative, are included for the insight they offer into the application of these teachings.

PART 1

FUNDAMENTAL PRINCIPLES OF RECONSTRUCTION

The role of agriculture is fundamental to the success of seemingly
unrelated processes as humankind advances toward a just and
unified society. Individuals and institutions have responsibility to
assist in the betterment of the world and the establishment of a
world-embracing peace. As administrative practices and spiritual
principles align, both public and private sectors recognize the
unique station of the farmer.

AGRICULTURE FIRST

Whilst in the Prison of 'Akká, We revealed in the Crimson Book that which is conducive to the advancement of mankind and to the reconstruction of the world. The utterances set forth therein by the Pen of the Lord of creation include the following which constitute the fundamental principles for the administration of the affairs of men:

First: It is incumbent upon the ministers of the House of Justice to promote the Lesser Peace so that the people of the earth may be relieved from the burden of exorbitant expenditures. This matter is imperative and absolutely essential, inasmuch as hostilities and conflict lie at the root of affliction and calamity.

Second: Languages must be reduced to one common language to be taught in all the schools of the world.

Third: It behooveth man to adhere tenaciously unto that which will promote fellowship, kindliness and unity.

Fourth: Everyone, whether man or woman, should hand over to a trusted person a portion of what he or she earneth through trade, agriculture or other occupation, for the training and education of children, to be spent for this purpose with the knowledge of the Trustees of the House of Justice.

Fifth: Special regard must be paid to agriculture. Although it hath been mentioned in the fifth place, unquestionably it precedeth the others. Agriculture is highly developed in foreign lands, however in Persia it hath so far been grievously neglected. It is hoped that His Majesty the Shah—may God assist him by His grace—will turn his attention to this vital and important matter. (Bahá'u'lláh, *Tablets of Bahá'u'lláh*, pp. 89–90)

The question of economics must commence with the farmer and then be extended to the other classes inasmuch as the number of farmers is far greater than all other classes. Therefore, it is fitting to begin with the farmer in matters related to economics for the farmer is the first active agent in human society. ('Abdu'l-Bahá, *Pearls of Bounty*, no. 2.21.1.)

And if, as thou passest by fields and plantations, thou observest that the plants, flowers and sweet-smelling herbs are growing luxuriantly together, forming a pattern of unity, this is an evidence of the fact that that plantation and garden is flourishing under the care of a skilled gardener. But when thou seest it in a state of disorder and irregularity thou inferrest that it hath lacked the training of an efficient farmer and thus hath produced weeds and tares. ('Abdu'l-Bahá, *Selections from the Writings of 'Abdu'l-Bahá*, no. 225.20)

If the land is deprived of a cultivator, it becomes a thicket of thriving weeds, but if a farmer is found to cultivate it, the resulting harvest provides sustenance for living things. It is therefore evident that the land is in need of the farmer's cultivation. ('Abdu'l-Bahá, *Some Answered Questions*, no. 3.2.)

First and foremost is the principle that to all the members of the body politic shall be given the greatest achievements of the world of humanity. Each one shall have the utmost welfare and well-being. To solve this problem we must begin with the farmer . . . ('Abdu'l-Bahá, *The Promulgation of Universal Peace*, p. 437)

For instance, the function of a gardener is to till the soil of the mineral kingdom and plant a tree which under his training and cultivation will attain perfection of growth. If it be wild and fruitless, it may be made fruitful and prolific by grafting. If small and unsightly, it will become lofty, beautiful and verdant under the gardener's training, whereas a tree bereft of his cultivation retrogresses daily, its fruit grows acrid and bitter as the trees of the jungle, or it may become entirely barren and bereft of its fruitage. ('Abdu'l-Bahá, *The Promulgation of Universal Peace*, p. 106)

The farmer must be accorded his or her rightful place in the processes of development and civilization building: as the villages are reconstructed, the cities will follow. (Bahá'í International Community, "Eradicating Poverty: Moving Forward as One," The Bahá'í International Community's Statement on Poverty, 14 February 2008)

Access to development programs and their benefits must be ensured for all. The economics of food production and distribution will have to be reoriented and the critical role of the farmer in food and economic security properly valued. (Bahá'í International Community, "Valuing Spirituality in Development: Initial Considerations Regarding the Creation of Spiritually Based Indicators for Development." A concept paper written for the World Faiths and Development Dialogue, Lambeth Palace, London, 18–19 February 1998)

SOME ELEMENTS OF RECONSTRUCTION

Whilst in the Prison of 'Akká, We revealed in the Crimson Book that which is conducive to the advancement of mankind and to the reconstruction of the world. (Bahá'u'lláh, *Tablets of Bahá'u'lláh*, p. 89)

Be anxiously concerned with the needs of the age ye live in, and center your deliberations on its exigencies and requirements. (Bahá'u'lláh, *Gleanings from the Writings of Bahá'u'lláh*, no. 106.1)

That which is conducive to the regeneration of the world and the salvation of the peoples and kindreds of the earth hath been sent down from the heaven of the utterance of Him Who is the Desire of the world. Give ye a hearing ear to the counsels of the Pen of Glory. Better is this for you than all that is on the earth. Unto this beareth witness My glorious and wondrous Book. (Bahá'u'lláh, *Tablets of Bahá'u'lláh*, p. 223)

In like manner all the members of the human family, whether peoples or governments, cities or villages, have become increasingly interdependent. For none is self-sufficiency any longer possible, inasmuch as political ties unite all peoples and nations, and the bonds of trade and industry, of agriculture and education, are being strengthened every day. Hence the unity of all mankind can in this day be achieved. Verily this is none other but one of the wonders of this wondrous age, this glorious century. ('Abdu'l-Bahá, *Selection from the Writings of 'Abdu'l-Bahá*, no. 15.6)

And among the teachings of Bahá'u'lláh is that religious, racial, political, economic and patriotic prejudices destroy the edifice of humanity. As long as these prejudices prevail, the world of humanity will not have rest. ('Abdu'l-Bahá, "First Tablet to The Hague," 17 December 1919, *Pearls of Bounty*, no. 2.1.11)

Today the benefits of universal peace are recognized amongst the people, and likewise the harmful effects of war are clear and manifest to all. But in this matter, knowledge alone is far from sufficient: A power of implementation is needed to establish it throughout the world. ('Abdu'l-Bahá, "Second Tablet to The Hague," 1 July 1920, *Pearls of Bounty*, no. 2.2.6)

First among the great principles revealed by Him is that of the investigation of reality. The meaning is that every individual member of humankind is exhorted and commanded to set aside superstitious beliefs, traditions and blind imitation of ancestral forms in religion and investigate reality for himself. Inasmuch as the fundamental reality is one, all religions and nations of the world will become one through investigation of reality. The announcement of this principle is not found in any of the sacred Books of the past. ('Abdu'l-Bahá, *The Promulgation of Universal Peace*, p. 610)

A fundamental teaching of Bahá'u'lláh is the oneness of the world of humanity. Addressing mankind, He says, "Ye are all leaves of one tree and the fruits of one branch." By this it is meant that the world of humanity is like a tree, the nations or peoples are the different limbs or branches of that tree, and the individual human creatures are as the fruits and blossoms thereof. In this way Bahá'u'lláh expressed the oneness of humankind. ('Abdu'l-Bahá, *The Promulgation of Universal Peace*, p. 640)

Let there be no mistake. The principle of the Oneness of Mankind—the pivot round which all the teachings of Bahá'u'lláh revolve—is no mere outburst of ignorant emotionalism or an expression of vague and pious hope. Its appeal is not to be merely identified with a reawakening of the spirit of brotherhood and good-will among men, nor does it aim solely at the fostering of harmonious cooperation among individual peoples and nations. Its implications are deeper, its claims greater than any which the Prophets of old were allowed to advance. Its message is applicable not only to the individual, but concerns itself primarily with the nature of those essential relationships that must bind all the states and nations as members of one human family. It does not constitute merely the enunciation of an ideal, but stands inseparably associated with an institution adequate to embody its truth, demonstrate its validity, and perpetuate its influence. It implies an organic change in the structure of present-day society, a change such as the world has not yet experienced. It constitutes a challenge, at once bold and universal, to outworn shibboleths of national creeds—creeds that have had their day and which must, in the ordinary course of events as shaped and controlled by Providence, give way to a new gospel, fundamentally different from, and infinitely superior to, what the world has already conceived. It calls for no less than the reconstruction and the demilitarization of the whole civilized world—a world organically unified in all the essential aspects of its life, its political machinery, its spiritual aspiration, its trade and finance, its script and language, and yet infinite in the diversity of the national characteristics of its federated units.

It represents the consummation of human evolution. (Shoghi Effendi, *The World Order of Bahá'u'lláh*, p. 42)

Adversity, prolonged, world wide, afflictive, allied to chaos and universal destruction, must needs convulse the nations, stir the conscience of the world, disillusion the masses, precipitate a radical change in the very conception of society, and coalesce ultimately the disjointed, the bleeding limbs of mankind into one body, single, organically united, and indivisible. (Shoghi Effendi, *The Promised Day is Come*, pp. 122–24)

Our world has entered the dark heart of an age of fundamental change beyond anything in all of its tumultuous history. Its peoples, of whatever race, nation, or religion, are being challenged to subordinate all lesser loyalties and limiting identities to their oneness as citizens of a single planetary homeland. In Bahá'u'lláh's words: "the well-being of mankind, its peace and security, are unattainable unless and until its unity is firmly established." (The Universal House of Justice, "Introduction," *The Kitáb-i-Aqdas*, p. 11)

. . . the concept of social and economic development is enshrined in the sacred Teachings of our Faith The beloved Master, through His illuminating words and deeds, set the example for the application of this concept to the reconstruction of society. (The Universal House of Justice, message dated 20 October 1983, to the Bahá'ís of the World)

His (Bahá'u'lláh's) assurance is engraved on every faithful heart: "The betterment of the world can be accomplished through pure and goodly deeds, through commendable and seemly conduct." (The Universal House of Justice, message dated 9 November 2018, to the Bahá'ís of the World)

As you know from your study of the Bahá'í writings, the principle that is to infuse all facets of organized life on the planet is the oneness of humankind, the hallmark of the age of maturity. That humanity constitutes a single people is a truth that, once viewed with scepticism, claims widespread acceptance today. The rejection of deeply ingrained prejudices and a growing sense of world citizenship are among the signs of this heightened awareness. Yet, however promising the rise in collective consciousness may be, it should be seen as only the first step of a process that will take decades—nay, centuries—to unfold. For the principle of the oneness of humankind, as proclaimed by Bahá'u'lláh, asks not merely for cooperation among people and nations. It calls for a complete reconceptualization of the relationships that sustain society. The deepening environmental crisis, driven by a system that condones the pillage of natural resources to satisfy an insatiable thirst for more, suggests how entirely inadequate is the present conception of humanity's relationship with nature; the deterioration of the home environment, with the accompanying rise in the systematic exploitation of women and children worldwide, makes clear how pervasive are the misbegotten notions that define relations within the family unit; the persistence of despotism, on the one hand, and the increasing disregard for authority, on the other, reveal how unsatisfactory to a maturing humanity is the current relationship between the individual and the institutions of society; the concentration of material wealth in the hands of a minority of the world's population gives an indication of how fundamentally ill-conceived are relationships among the many sectors of what is now an emerging global community. The principle of the oneness of humankind implies, then, an organic change in the very structure of society. (The Universal House of Justice, message dated 2 March 2013, to the Bahá'ís of Iran)

"Regard the world as the human body," wrote Bahá'u'lláh to Queen Victoria. We can surely regard the Bahá'í world, the army of God, in the same way. In the human body, every cell, every organ, every nerve has its part to play. When all do so the body is healthy, vigorous, radiant, ready for every call made upon it. No cell, however humble, lives apart from the body, whether in serving it or receiving from it. This is true of the body of mankind in which God "hast endowed each and all with talents and faculties," and is supremely true of the body of the Bahá'í World Community, for this body is already an organism, united in its aspirations, unified in its methods, seeking assistance and confirmation from the same Source, and illumined with the conscious knowledge of its unity. (The Universal House of Justice, message dated September 1964, to the Bahá'ís of the World)

Although Bahá'u'lláh does not set out in His Revelation a detailed economic system, a constant theme throughout the entire corpus of His teachings is the reorganization of human society. Consideration of this theme inevitably gives rise to questions of economics. Of course, the future order conceived by Bahá'u'lláh is far beyond anything that can be imagined by the present generation. Nevertheless, its eventual emergence will depend on strenuous effort by His followers to put His teachings into effect today. . . . (The Universal House of Justice, message dated March 2017, to the Bahá'ís of the World)

Bahá'ís are encouraged to see in the revolutionary changes taking place in every sphere of life the interaction of two fundamental processes. One is destructive in nature, while the other is integrative; both serve to carry humanity, each in its own way, along the path leading towards its full maturity. The operation of the former is everywhere apparent—in the vicissitudes that have afflicted time-honoured institutions, in the impotence of leaders at all levels to mend the fractures appearing in the structure of society, in the dismantling of social norms that have long held in check unseemly passions, and in the despondency and indifference exhibited not only by individuals but also by entire societies that have lost any vital sense of purpose. Though devastating in their effects, the forces of disintegration tend to sweep away barriers that block humanity's progress, opening space for the process of integration to draw diverse groups together and disclosing new opportunities for cooperation and collaboration. Bahá'ís, of course, strive to align themselves, individually and collectively, with forces associated with the process of integration, which, they are confident, will continue to gain in strength, no matter how bleak the immediate horizons. Human affairs will be utterly reorganized, and an era of universal peace inaugurated. Such is the view of history that underlies every endeavour pursued by the Bahá'í community. (The Universal House of Justice, message dated 2 March 2013, to the Bahá'ís of Iran)

What should be stated plainly here is that Bahá'ís do not believe the transformation thus envisioned will come about exclusively through their own efforts. Nor are they trying to create a movement that would seek to impose on society their vision of the future. Every nation and every group—indeed, every individual—will, to a greater or lesser degree, contribute to the emergence of the world civilization towards which humanity is irresistibly moving. Unity will progressively be achieved, as foreshadowed by 'Abdu'l-Bahá, in different realms of social existence, for instance, "unity in the political realm," "unity of thought in world undertakings," "unity of races" and the "unity of nations." As these come to be realized, the structures of a politically united world, which respects the full diversity of culture and provides channels for the expression of dignity and honour, will gradually take shape. (The Universal House of Justice, message dated 2 March 2013, to the Bahá'ís of Iran)

The second fundamental principle which enables us to understand the pattern towards which Bahá'u'lláh wishes human society to evolve is the principle of organic growth which requires that detailed developments, and the understanding of detailed developments, become available only with the passage of time and with the help of the guidance given by that Central Authority in the Cause to whom all must turn. In this regard one can use the simile of a tree. If a farmer plants a tree, he cannot state at that moment what its exact height will be, the number of its branches or the exact time of its blossoming. He can, however, give a general impression of its size and pattern of growth and can state with confidence which fruit it will bear. The same is true of the evolution of the World Order of Bahá'u'lláh. (From a letter written on behalf of the Universal House of Justice, dated 27 April 1995, to an individual)

One of the most pressing problems of humanity in the current century is how a growing, rapidly developing, and not yet united global population can, in a just manner, live in harmony with the planet and its finite resources. Certain biological realities present themselves when an organism negatively affects or exceeds the capacity of its ecosystem. The limited availability and inequitable distribution of resources profoundly impact social relations within and between nations in many ways, even to the point of precipitating upheaval and war. And particular arrangements of human affairs can have devastating consequences for the environment. The question of the impact of climate change, and to what extent it is man-made and its effects can be ameliorated, is today a major aspect of this larger problem. The Revelation of Bahá'u'lláh directly and indirectly touches on a range of such concerns in a manner that speaks to a harmony between society and the natural world. It is essential, therefore, that Bahá'ís contribute to thought and action regarding such matters. (From a letter written on behalf of the Universal House of Justice, dated 29 November 2017, to three individuals)

Every development effort can be said to represent a response to some understanding of the nature and state of society, its challenges, the institutions operating in it, the forces influencing it, and the capacities of its peoples. To read society in this way is not to explore every detail of the social reality. Nor does it necessarily involve formal studies. Conditions need to be understood progressively, both from the perspective of a particular endeavour's purpose and in the context of a vision of humanity's collective existence. Indeed, it is vital that the reading of society be consistent with the teachings of the Faith. That the true nature of a human being is spiritual, that every human being is a "mine rich in gems" of limitless potential, that the forces of integration and disintegration each in their own way are propelling humanity towards its destiny are but a few examples of teachings that would shape one's understanding of social reality. (*Social Action*. A paper prepared by the Office of Social and Economic Development at the Bahá'í World Center, 26 November 2012)

Central to the capacity of a Bahá'í community to lead a process of transformation is the ability of its members and institutions to apply the Revelation of Bahá'u'lláh to various aspects of life and thereby establish consistent patterns of change. In fact, learning to apply the Teachings to achieve progress could be taken as the very definition of Bahá'í social and economic development. Such learning has to occur locally, regionally, nationally and internationally and become the axis around which our development efforts are organized at all levels. Learning in this sense is not limited to study and evaluation. It comes about in combination with action. ("Bahá'í Social And Economic Development: Prospects for the Future," 16 September 1993. A statement approved by The Universal House of Justice for use in orienting and guiding the work of Bahá'í social and economic development throughout the world)

Justice is the one power that can translate the dawning consciousness of humanity's oneness into a collective will through which the necessary structures of global community life can be confidently erected. . . . At the individual level, justice is that faculty of the human soul that enables each person to distinguish truth from falsehood. . . . At a group level, a concern for justice is the indispensable compass in the collective decision making, because it is the only means by which unity of thought and action can be achieved. (*The Prosperity of Humankind.* A statement prepared by the Bahá'í International Community Office of Public Information, Haifa, 1995)

These rising impulses for change must be seized upon and channeled into overcoming the remaining barriers that block realization of the age-old dream of global peace. The effort of will required for such a task cannot be summoned up merely by appeals for action against countless ills afflicting society. It must be galvanized by a vision of human prosperity in the fullest sense of the term—an awakening to the possibilities of the spiritual and material well-being now brought within grasp. Its beneficiaries must be all of the planet's inhabitants, without distinction, without the imposition of conditions unrelated to the fundamental goals of such a reorganization of human affairs. (*The Prosperity of Humankind.* A statement prepared by the Bahá'í International Community Office of Public Information, Haifa, 1995)

Much has been said about the need for cooperation to solve a climate challenge that no nation or community can solve alone. The principle of the oneness of humankind . . . seeks to move beyond utilitarian notions of cooperation to anchor the aspirations of individuals, communities and nations to those of the progress of humanity. In practical terms, it affirms that individual and national interests are best served in tandem with the progress of the whole. As children, women, men, religious and scientific communities as well as governments and international institutions converge on this reality, we will do more than achieve a collective response to the climate change crisis. We will usher in a new paradigm by means of which we can understand our purpose and responsibilities in an interconnected world; a new standard by which to evaluate human progress; and a mode of governance faithful to the ties that bind us as members of one human race. (Bahá'í International Community, "Seizing the Opportunity: Redefining the challenge of climate change, Initial Considerations of the Bahá'í International Community," 1 December 2008)

While it is acknowledged that any effective climate change policy needs to be rooted in a global perspective, even this enlargement of the sphere of responsibility has not sufficiently moved governments to act. This perspective must now evolve to reflect the essential connectedness and common fate of humanity that for too long has struggled against a worldview that emphasized sovereignty, ascendancy and competition. Efforts to reconceptualize sovereignty, from an absolute right to a responsibility, signal that a shift in consciousness towards greater degrees of global solidarity is already underway. (Bahá'í International Community, "Seizing the Opportunity: Redefining the challenge of climate change, Initial Considerations of the Bahá'í International Community," 1 December 2008)

Development must be decentralized in order to involve communities in formulating and implementing the decisions and programs that affect their lives. Such a decentralization need not conflict with a global system and strategy, but would in fact ensure that developmental processes are adapted to the planet's rich cultural, geographic, and ecological diversity. (Bahá'í International Community, "Earth Charter," 5 April 1991. The following statement offering suggestions for the proposed "Earth Charter," was originally presented by the Bahá'í International Community to the Preparatory Committee of the United Nations Conference on Environment and Development (UNCED), June 1992)

A core element of a strategy of sustainable development is the reform of agricultural policies and processes. Food production and agriculture is the world's single largest source of employment; nearly 70% of the poor in developing countries live in rural areas and depend on agriculture for their livelihoods. Although farming has been devalued by manufacturing and a rapidly expanding urban population, agriculture still represents the fundamental basis of economic and community life: malnourishment and food insecurity suffocate all attempts at development and progress. Despite this pivotal role, poverty is often concentrated in rural areas. Damage to natural resources, poor information and infrastructure often result in food insecurity, premature deaths and mass migration to urban areas in search of a better life. The farmer must be accorded his or her rightful place in the processes of development and civilization building: as the villages are reconstructed, the cities will follow. (Bahá'í International Community, "Eradicating Poverty: Moving Forward as One," The Bahá'í International Community's Statement on Poverty, 14 February 2008)

A rich and deepening consciousness of the oneness of humankind is the only way that the obstacles inherent in dichotomies like rich/poor, north/south, developed/developing can be overcome. Designations of this kind are not without basis, for some countries *do* have more financial resources than others. But while such realities are not to be denied, neither should they be allowed to paralyze constructive action. Rather, they should be incorporated into the perspective that an integrated, sustainable and prosperous world will not be built by "us" working together with "them," but by all of us working on behalf of everyone. (Bahá'í International Community, "Shared Vision, Shared Volition: Choosing Our Global Future Together," a statement of the Bahá'í International Community to the United Nations Climate Change Conference in Paris, France, 23 November 2015)

For Bahá'ís, Bahá'u'lláh's promise that civilization will exist on this planet for a minimum of five thousand centuries makes it unconscionable to ignore the long-term impact of decisions made today. (Bahá'í International Community, "Conservation and Sustainable Development in the Bahá'í Faith," paper presented by the Bahá'í International Community to the Summit on the Alliance Between Religions and Conservation, 3 May 1995)

PROTAGONISTS

It behooveth man to adhere tenaciously unto that which will promote fellowship, kindliness and unity. (Bahá'u'lláh, *Tablets of Bahá'u'lláh*, p. 90)

The effects of this systematic approach to human resource development are making themselves felt in the lives of all three protagonists of the Plan—the individual believer, the institutions, and the local community. (The Universal House of Justice, message dated 26 November 1999, to the Bahá'ís of the World)

Every follower of Bahá'u'lláh knows well that the purpose of His Revelation is to bring into being a new creation. No sooner had "the First Call gone forth from His lips than the whole creation was revolutionized, and all that are in the heavens and all that are on earth were stirred to the depths." The individual, the institutions, and the community—the three protagonists in the Divine Plan—are being shaped under the direct influence of His Revelation, and a new conception of each, appropriate for a humanity that has come of age, is emerging. The relationships that bind them, too, are undergoing a profound transformation, bringing into the realm of existence civilization-building powers which can only be released through conformity with His decree. (The Universal House of Justice, message dated 28 December 2010, to the Conference of the Continental Board of Counsellors)

When society is in such difficulty and distress, the responsibility of the Bahá'ís to make a constructive contribution to human affairs becomes more pronounced. This is a moment when distinct but interrelated lines of action converge upon a single point, when the call to service rings aloud. The individual, the community, and the institutions of the Faith—inseparable protagonists in the advancement of civilization—are in a position to demonstrate the distinctive features of the Bahá'í way of life, characterized by increased maturity in the discharge of their responsibilities and in their relationships with each other. They are summoned to a fuller expression of the Faith's society-building powers. Agencies and projects dedicated to social action may have to adapt their approaches in order to meet expanded needs; efforts to do this are sure to infuse ongoing programmes with deeper meaning and purpose. Further, Bahá'í contributions to discourses newly prevalent in society are generating heightened interest, and there is a responsibility to be discharged here too. At a time when the urgency of attaining higher levels of unity, founded on the incontestable truth of humanity's oneness, is becoming apparent to larger and larger numbers, society stands in need of clear voices that can articulate the spiritual principles that underlie such an aspiration. (The Universal House of Justice, message dated 9 May 2020, to all National Spiritual Assemblies)

The building of capacity in individuals and institutions goes hand in hand with the development of communities. In villages and neighbourhoods throughout the world, Bahá'ís are engaged in activities that enrich the devotional character of their communities, that tend to the spiritual education of children, that enhance the spiritual perception of junior youth and strengthen their powers of expression, and that enable increasing numbers to explore the application of the teachings of the Faith to their individual and collective lives. A process of community development, however, needs to reach beyond the level of activity and concern itself with those modes of expression and patterns of thought and behaviour that are to characterize a humanity which has come of age. In short, it must enter into the realm of culture. Viewed in this light, social action can become an occasion to raise collective consciousness of such vital principles as oneness, justice, and the equality of women and men; to promote an environment distinguished by traits such as truthfulness, equity, trustworthiness, and generosity; to enhance the ability of a community to resist the influence of destructive social forces; to demonstrate the value of cooperation as an organizing principle for activity; to fortify collective volition; and to infuse practice with insight from the teachings. For, in the final analysis, many of the questions most central to the emergence of a prosperous global civilization are to be addressed at the level of culture.

What seems necessary to acknowledge here is that the increase of capacity in each of these three protagonists does not occur in isolation; the development of any one is inextricably linked to the progress of the other two. The following statement of Shoghi Effendi speaks to this point:

"We cannot segregate the human heart from the environment outside us and say that once one of these is reformed everything will be improved. Man is organic with the world. His inner life moulds the environment and is itself also deeply affected by it. The one acts upon the other and every abiding change in the life of man is the result of these mutual reactions." (*Social Action*. A paper prepared by the Office of Social and Economic Development at the Bahá'í World Center, 26 November 2012)

Endowed with the wealth of all the genetic and cultural diversity that has evolved through past ages, the earth's inhabitants are now challenged to draw on their collective inheritance to take up, consciously and systematically, the responsibility for the design of their future. (*The Prosperity of Humankind.* A statement prepared by the Bahá'í International Community Office of Public Information, Haifa, 1995)

In essence, the view of the Bahá'í International Community is that individual and social values are fundamental to the fostering of rural development. Such a view does not discount the importance of appropriate technology, nor does it seek to minimize the importance of economic and administrative measures. However, it does hold that individual attitudes are the key to enduring development and that these attitudes are a natural consequence of spiritual values. (Bahá'í International Community, "Spiritual and Social Values for Rural Development," paper presented to the Twentieth Conference of the South Pacific Commission Port Moresby, Papua New Guinea, 18 October 1980)

It is now increasingly acknowledged that such conditions as the marginalization of girls and women, poor governance, ethnic and religious antipathy, environmental degradation and unemployment constitute formidable obstacles to the progress and development of communities. These evidence a deeper crisis—one rooted in the values and attitudes that shape relationships at all levels of society. Viewed from this perspective, poverty can be described as the absence of those ethical, social and material resources needed to develop the moral, intellectual and social capacities of individuals, communities and institutions. Moral reasoning, group decision-making and freedom from racism, for example, are all essential tools for poverty alleviation. Such capacities must shape individual thinking as well as institutional arrangements and policy-making. To be clear, the goal at hand is not only to remove the ills of poverty but to engage the masses of humanity in the construction of a just global order. (Bahá'í International Community, "Eradicating Poverty: Moving Forward as One," The Bahá'í International Community's Statement on Poverty, 14 February 2008)

Exploring new patterns of interaction among the actors of society, such as individuals and institutions, will be central to the task of building more sustainable relationships with the natural world and among various segments of the global family. The work of addressing global climate change ultimately revolves around the aim of human lives well lived, which is a goal cherished by people and cultures the world over. In it can therefore be found a powerful point of unity to support the work ahead. We trust that the efforts of those at COP 21 will contribute to building a firm foundation on which the well-being and prosperity of humanity can be ever more effectively pursued for this and future generations. (Bahá'í International Community, "Shared Vision, Shared Volition: Choosing Our Global Future Together," a statement of the Bahá'í International Community to the United Nations Climate Change Conference in Paris, France, 23 November 2015)

The Bahá'í International Community has been addressing environmental issues and, more specifically, climate change for several years. It has worked for more than two decades to contribute to discourses on issues related to the environment. This plan describes the approach the Bahá'í community proposes to educate our community about climate change, to raise consciousness about environmental issues and to build the capacity of our members to contribute to the resolution of this global challenge. The plan reflects certain general principles that are important for the Bahá'í community. Bahá'ís believe that progress in the development field depends on and is driven by stirrings at the grass roots of society rather than from an imposition of externally developed plans and programmes. This plan, then seeks to increase local communities' and individuals' awareness of the needs and possibilities and of their capacity to respond. Different communities will likely devise different approaches and solutions in response to similar needs. It is for each community to determine its goals and priorities in keeping with its capacity and resources. Given the diversity of communities around the world, the plan encourages innovation and a variety of approaches to the environment appropriate to the rhythm of life in the community. The commitment to preserve the autonomy and diversity of Bahá'í communities does not take away from the unity of the worldwide Bahá'í community. In fact, Bahá'í s all over the world are engaged in a coherent framework of action that promotes the spiritual development of the individual and channels the collective energies of its members towards service to humanity. Thousands upon thousands of Bahá'ís, embracing the diversity of the entire human family, are engaged in certain core activities. These activities promote the systematic study of the Bahá'í Writings in small groups in order to build capacity for service. They respond to the inmost longing of every heart to commune with its Maker by carrying out acts of collective worship in diverse settings, uniting with others in prayer, awakening spiritual susceptibilities, and shaping a pattern of life distinguished for its devotional character. They provide for the needs of the children of the world and offer them lessons that develop their spiritual faculties and lay the foundations of a noble and upright character. They also assist junior youth to navigate through a crucial stage of their lives and to become empowered to direct their energies toward the advancement of civilization. As Bahá'ís and their friends gain experience with these initiatives, an increasing number are able to express their faith through a rising tide of endeavours that address the needs of humanity in both their spiritual and material dimensions. To carry out such a massive enterprise Regional Institutes have been created throughout the world over several decades. This capacity building process at the grass roots level with individuals assists them to serve as tutors of study circles, teachers of children's classes and facilitators of junior youth empowerment programs. The approach to curriculum development followed by the Institute is not the traditional one of design, field-testing and evaluation, carried out in a linear fashion. The first step in writing any set of materials is taken, rather, when an experience is created at the grassroots in performing some act of service in response to the exigencies of the development of a community. Materials emerge out of this experience and become an expression of it. They are, on the one hand, a record of the learning that occurs in applying the Bahá'í Writings in a particular area of service and, on the other, an instrument for the systematization of that learning. These materials are used and then further refined and revised based on experience. As suggested by the foregoing, the Institute's courses are not arranged according to a series of subject matters, with the specific aim of increasing individual knowledge. The content and order are based, rather, on a series of acts of service, the practice of which creates capacity in the individual to meet the exigencies of dynamic, developing communities. The enhancement of such capacity is viewed in terms of "walking a path of service." On such a path individuals are assisted first in accomplishing relatively simple tasks and then in performing more complex and demanding acts of service. (Bahá'í International Community, "Bahá'í International Community's Plan of Action on Climate Change," 2009)

Much has been said about the need for cooperation to solve a climate challenge that no nation or community can solve alone. The principle of the oneness of humankind . . . seeks to move beyond utilitarian notions of cooperation to anchor the aspirations of individuals, communities and nations to those of the progress of humanity. In practical terms, it affirms that individual and national interests are best served in tandem with the progress of the whole. As children, women, men, religious and scientific communities as well as governments and international institutions converge on this reality, we will do more than achieve a collective response to the climate change crisis. We will usher in a new paradigm by means of which we can understand our purpose and responsibilities in an interconnected world; a new standard by which to evaluate human progress; and a mode of governance faithful to the ties that bind us as members of one human race. (Bahá'í International Community, "Seizing the Opportunity: Redefining the challenge of climate change, Initial Considerations of the Bahá'í International Community," 1 December 2008)

Anthropogenic climate change is not inevitable; humanity chooses its relationships with the natural world. . . . The current global order has often approached the natural world as a reservoir of material resources to be exploited. The grave consequences of this paradigm have become all too apparent, and more balanced relationships among the peoples of the world and the planet are clearly needed. The question today is how new patterns of action and interaction can best be established, both individually and collectively, through personal choices, social systems, and governing institutions. (Bahá'í International Community, "Shared Vision, Shared Volition: Choosing Our Global Future Together," a statement of the Bahá'í International Community to the United Nations Climate Change Conference in Paris, France, 23 November 2015)

Action on issues of sustainability is often grounded in the sentiment that we all live on the same planet. Of course shared concerns such as climate change, transnational migration, and global pandemics are not to be discounted. But truly transforming individual and collective patterns of life will require a much deeper appreciation of the interconnectedness of the planetary biosphere. People and the environment are inter-connected aspects of one organically integrated system. At this point in history, neither can be accurately understood in isolation from the other. (Bahá'í International Community, "Shared Vision, Shared Volition: Choosing Our Global Future Together," a statement of the Bahá'í International Community to the United Nations Climate Change Conference in Paris, France, 23 November 2015)

The principle of the oneness of humankind has implications for relationships at all levels. Individual choices and governmental action are often subtly placed in opposition to one another, suggesting that one or the other either takes or deserves precedence. In reality, of course, both are needed. Agreements and protocols at the governmental level will not be sufficient if individuals do not adopt more sustainable lifestyles and behaviors. Similarly, individual actions alone, such as conserving water and reducing waste, for instance, will not be sufficient if governments do not make the necessary changes at the structural level. Also crucial is the community which, as a distinct unit of civilization with its own capacities and qualities, has a unique and vital role that cannot be overlooked. Increasing integration between these three levels will be needed, if long-lasting progress is to be achieved (Bahá'í International Community, "Shared Vision, Shared Volition: Choosing Our Global Future Together," a statement of the Bahá'í International Community to the United Nations Climate Change Conference in Paris, France, 23 November 2015)

INDIVIDUALS

All men have been created to carry forward an ever-advancing civilization. (Bahá'u'lláh, *Gleanings from the Writings of Bahá'u'lláh*, no. 109.2)

Great is the station of man. Great must also be his endeavors for the rehabilitation of the world and the well-being of nations. I beseech the One true God to graciously confirm thee in that which beseemeth man's station. (Bahá'u'lláh, *Tablets of Bahá'u'lláh*, p. 11)

We love to see you at all times consorting in amity and concord within the paradise of My good-pleasure, and to inhale from your acts the fragrance of friendliness and unity, of loving-kindness and fellowship. Thus counseleth you the All-Knowing, the Faithful. (Bahá'u'lláh, *Gleanings from the Writings of Bahá'u'lláh*, no. 146.1)

O people of Bahá! It is incumbent upon each one of you to engage in some occupation—such as a craft, a trade or the like. We have exalted your engagement in such work to the rank of worship of the one true God. (Bahá'u'lláh, The Kitáb-i-Aqdas, ¶33)

It is incumbent upon everyone, even should he be a resident in a particular land for no more than a single day, to become engaged in some craft or trade, or agriculture, and that the very pursuit of such a calling is, in the eyes of the one true God, identical with worship. (Bahá'u'lláh, from a Tablet to an individual believer, in Universal House of Justice, Research Department, *Economics, Agriculture and Related Subjects*, p. 1)

All the friends of God . . . should contribute to the extent possible, however modest their offering may be. God doth not burden a soul beyond its capacity. Such contributions must come from all centers and all believers. . . . O Friends of God! Be ye assured that in place of these contributions your agriculture, your industry, and your commerce will be blessed by manifold increases, with goodly gifts and bestowals. He who cometh with one goodly deed will receive a tenfold reward. There is no doubt that the living Lord will abundantly confirm those who expend their wealth in His path. ('Abdu'l-Bahá, from a Tablet translated from the Persian, Universal House of Justice, Research Department, *Agriculture and Rural Life*, 1995)

One of Bahá'u'lláh's teachings is the adjustment of means of livelihood in human society. Under this adjustment there can be no extremes in human conditions as regards wealth and sustenance. For the community needs financier, farmer, merchant and laborer just as an army must be composed of commander, officers and privates. All cannot be commanders; all cannot be officers or privates. Each in his station in the social fabric must be competent—each in his function according to ability but with justness of opportunity for all. ('Abdu'l-Bahá, *The Promulgation of Universal Peace*, p. 302)

With reference to Bahá'u'lláh's command concerning the engagement of the believers in some sort of profession: the Teachings are most emphatic on this matter, particularly the statement in the Aqdas to this effect which makes it quite clear that idle people who lack the desire to work can have no place in the new World Order. . . . Every individual, no matter how handicapped and limited he may be, is under the obligation of engaging in some work or profession, for work, especially when performed in the spirit of service, is according to Bahá'u'lláh a form of worship. It has not only a utilitarian purpose, but has a value in itself, because it draws us nearer to God, and enables us to better grasp His purpose for us in this world. It is obvious, therefore, that the inheritance of wealth cannot make anyone immune from daily work. (Shoghi Effendi, in *The Kitáb-i-Aqdas*, Notes, p. 33)

It is the duty of those who are in charge of the organization of society to give every individual the opportunity of acquiring the necessary talent in some kind of profession, and also the means of utilizing such a talent, both for its own sake and for the sake of earning the means of his livelihood. (From a letter written on behalf of Shoghi Effendi, dated 22 March 1937, to the National Spiritual Assembly of the United States and Canada)

In one of His Tablets, 'Abdu'l-Bahá states that "if a person is incapable of earning a living, is stricken by dire poverty or becometh helpless, then it is incumbent on the wealthy or the Deputies to provide him with a monthly allowance for his subsistence. . . . By 'Deputies' is meant the representatives of the people, that is to say the members of the House of Justice." (The Universal House of Justice, in *The Kitáb-i-Aqdas*, Notes, no. 56)

When the question of National Service, such as you describe in Guyana, includes training in skills and professions useful to mankind, such as agriculture, the friends may certainly volunteer for such services, provided they are definitely assured that their training will not subject them later to call up for military service in combatant roles. (The Universal House of Justice, message dated 14 September 1975, to the National Spiritual Assembly of Guyana, Surinam and French Guiana)

Man, possessed of an inner faculty which plants and animals do not have, a power which enables him to discover the secrets of nature and gain mastery over the environment, has a special responsibility to use his God-given powers for positive ends. The Universal House of Justice indicates that "the proper exercise of this responsibility is the key to whether his inventive genius produces beneficial results, or creates havoc in the material world." (From a letter written on behalf of the Universal House of Justice, dated 19 May 1971, to an individual believer)

At the level of the individual, the influence of the training institute is vital. As it helps to equip individuals with the spiritual insights and knowledge, the qualities and attitudes, and the skills and abilities needed to carry out acts of service integral to Bahá'í community life, the institute creates a pool of human resources that makes it possible for endeavours of social and economic development to flourish. The participants in such endeavours are able to acquire, in turn, knowledge and skills pertinent to the specific areas of action in which they are engaged—health, agricultural production, and education, to name but a few—while continuing to strengthen those capacities already cultivated by the institute, for instance, fostering unity in diversity, promoting justice, participating effectively in consultation, and accompanying others in their efforts to serve humanity. (*Social Action*. A paper prepared by the Office of Social and Economic Development at the Bahá'í World Center, 26 November 2012)

Only a comprehensive vision of a global society, supported by universal values and principles, can inspire individuals to take responsibility for the long-term care and protection of the natural environment. Bahá'ís find such a world-embracing vision and system of values in the teachings of Bahá'u'lláh—teachings which herald an era of planetary justice, prosperity and unity. (Bahá'í International Community, "Conservation and Sustainable Development in the Bahá'í Faith," paper presented by the Bahá'í International Community to the Summit on the Alliance between Religions and Conservation, 3 May 1995)

Individuals and institutions must work in tandem to take up this task. One of the goals of poverty alleviation, then, centers on the individual: he must be helped to reclaim his dignity and sense of self-worth, must be encouraged to gain confidence to improve his condition and strive to realize his potential. Beyond the achievement of personal well-being, he must be nurtured to become a source of social good—of peace, happiness and advantage to those around him. It is at the level of service to others that our humanity achieves its highest expression. (Bahá'í International Community, "Eradicating Poverty: Moving Forward as One," The Bahá'í International Community's Statement on Poverty, 14 February 2008)

A large share of the responsibility for poverty eradication rests with the individuals themselves. While poverty is the product of numerous factors: historic, economic, political and environmental, there is also a cultural dimension, which manifests itself in individual values and attitudes. Some of these—such as the subjugation of girls and women, the lack of value of education or of an individual's right to progress—can exacerbate conditions of poverty. (Bahá'í International Community, "Eradicating Poverty: Moving Forward as One," The Bahá'í International Community's Statement on Poverty, 14 February 2008)

Women

And among the teachings of Bahá'u'lláh is the equality of women and men. The world of humanity has two wings—one is women and the other men. Not until both wings are equally developed can the bird fly. Should one wing remain weak, flight is impossible. Not until the world of women becomes equal to the world of men in the acquisition of virtues and perfections, can success and prosperity be attained as they ought to be. ('Abdu'l-Bahá, *Selections from the Writings of 'Abdu'l-Bahá,* no. 227.18)

In some respects woman is superior to man. She is more tenderhearted, more receptive, her intuition is more intense. ('Abdu'l-Bahá, *Paris Talks,* no. 50.6)

Woman must especially devote her energies and abilities toward the industrial and agricultural sciences, seeking to assist mankind in that which is most needful. By this means she will demonstrate capability and ensure recognition of equality in the social and economic equation. ('Abdu'l-Bahá, *The Promulgation of Universal Peace,* p. 395)

. . . it is well established in history that where woman has not participated in human affairs the outcomes have never attained a state of completion and perfection." ('Abdu'l-Bahá, *The Promulgation of Universal Peace,* p. 185)

The woman is indeed of the greater importance to the race. She has the greater burden and the greater work. Look at the vegetable and the animal worlds. The palm which carries the fruit is the tree most prized by the date grower. The Arab knows that for a long journey the mare has the longest wind. For her greater strength and fierceness, the lioness is more feared by the hunter than the lion. . . . The woman has greater moral courage than the man; she has also special gifts which enable her to govern in moments of danger and crisis. ('Abdu'l-Bahá, *'Abdu'l-Bahá in London,* pp. 102–3)

Woman by nature is opposed to war; she is an advocate of peace. . . . Consider, for instance, a mother who has tenderly reared a son for twenty years to the age of maturity. Surely she will not consent to having that son torn asunder and killed in the field of battle. Therefore, as woman advances toward the degree of man in power and privilege, with the right of vote and control in human government, most assuredly war will cease; for woman is naturally the most devoted and staunch advocate of international peace. ('Abdu'l-Bahá, *The Promulgation of Universal Peace,* p. 529)

The emancipation of women, the achievement of full equality between the sexes, is one of the most important, though less acknowledged prerequisites of peace. The denial of such equality perpetrates an injustice against one half of the world's population and promotes in men harmful attitudes and habits that are carried from the family to the workplace, to political life, and ultimately to international relations. There are no grounds, moral, practical, or biological, upon which such denial can be justified. Only as women are welcomed into full partnership in all fields of human endeavor will the moral and psychological climate be created in which international peace can emerge. (The Universal House of Justice, message dated October 1985, to the Peoples of the World)

A further extract about women and peace is taken from a letter written on behalf of the Guardian on 24 March 1945: What 'Abdu'l-Bahá meant about the women arising for peace is that this is a matter which vitally affects women, and when they form a conscious and overwhelming mass of public opinion against war there can be no war. (From a letter written on behalf of the Universal House of Justice, dated 5 January 1986, to an individual)

. . . discrimination against women remains the most widespread injustice in the world today. (Bahá'í International Community, "Toward a New Discourse on Religion and Gender Equality," 1 February 2015)

It does not seem possible to overestimate the extent to which rural development would be fostered by full implementation of the principle of equality of rights, privileges and opportunities for both sexes. The rational powers and creative energies of one-half of the population, so far neglected, would then be developed and brought to bear on the problems of rural life. In purely practical terms, co-operation between two equals united by a marriage bond is far more productive than the unequal relationship which exists wherever women are regarded as inferior. The education of women, and their encouragement, has the further effect of implanting in the minds of the children entrusted to their care an appreciation for literacy and mental development as well as a facility for innovation. (Bahá'í International Community, "Spiritual and Social Values for Rural Development," paper presented to the Twentieth Conference of the South Pacific Commission Port Moresby, Papua New Guinea, 18 October 1980)

Youth

Thy letter was received. Praise be to God it imparted the good news of thy health and safety and indicated that thou art ready to enter an agricultural school. This is highly suitable. Strive as much as possible to become proficient in the science of agriculture, for in accordance with the divine teachings the acquisition of sciences and the perfection of arts are considered acts of worship. If a man engageth with all his power in the acquisition of a science or in the perfection of an art, it is as if he has been worshipping God in churches and temples. Thus as thou enterest a school of agriculture and strivest in the acquisition of that science thou art day and night engaged in acts of worship—acts that are accepted at the threshold of the Almighty. ('Abdu'l-Bahá, *Selections from the Writings of 'Abdu'l-Bahá*, no. 126.1)

Since thy dear child is taking his examinations, my fervent wish at the divine Threshold is that, by the grace and favour of God, he may meet with success, and that in the future he may go on to study agriculture and master its various branches, practical and theoretical. Agriculture is a noble science and, should thy son become proficient in this field, he will become a means of providing for the comfort of untold numbers of people. ('Abdu'l-Bahá, Tablet to an individual believer, *Extracts from the Bahá'í Writings on the Subject of Agriculture and Related Subjects.* Universal House of Justice Research Department. Revised 12 November 2001)

Let Bahá'í youth, therefore, consider the best ways in which they can use and develop their native abilities for the service of mankind and the Cause of God, whether this be as farmers, teachers, doctors, artisans, musicians or any one of the multitude of livelihoods that are open to them. (The Universal House of Justice, message dated 10 June 1966, To the Bahá'í Youth in every Land)

So fundamental are these duties and obligations that to some degree all entities—youth, parents, Bahá'í institutions—share in them, acting in accordance with their respective functions and responsibilities. There is a sphere in which each must make independent judgments and take independent action. A youth must decide on what professional training to pursue and keep a balance between such pursuit and his spiritual obligations; the parents must assist the youth, through material support and moral guidance, to achieve his goal, and must also encourage the youth in the observance of his spiritual obligations; the institutions must promote the Cause of God, endeavor to stimulate action on the part of individual believers in the teaching and consolidation of the Faith, with the full realization that if such action is neglected there can be no hope for the peace of mankind and the future growth of civilization. The institutions cannot, therefore, fail to urge the friends to service and to call their attention to the critical situation of the times and to point out the crucial importance of the action of the individual to the fortunes of the Faith and humanity as a whole. (The Universal House of Justice, letter dated 28 October 1992, to two individuals)

When deciding what course of training to follow, youth can consider acquiring those skills and professions that will be of benefit in education, rural development, agriculture, economics, technology, health, radio and in many other areas of endeavour that are so urgently needed in the developing countries of the world. (The Universal House of Justice, message dated July 4, 1983, to the European Youth Conference in Innsbruck)

The youth face the pressing obligation of completing their education so as to acquire a profession or trade while at the same time observing their other spiritual obligations and duties to God. (The Universal House of Justice, 28 October 1992, to two individuals)

As important as it is for parents to exercise their moral authority in assisting the youth not to make unwise decisions, it is also incumbent on the parents as Bahá'ís to give due consideration to the significance of the spiritual impact of the Faith upon the youth and recognize that the youth must have some latitude to respond to the stirrings of their hearts and souls, since they, beginning at the age of 15, must assume serious spiritual obligations and duties and are themselves alone ultimately responsible to God for the progress of their own souls. (The Universal House of Justice, letter dated 28 October 1992, to two individuals)

Recent events call to mind heart-rending episodes in the history of the Faith, of cruel deceptions wrought against your forebears. It is only appropriate that you strive to transcend the opposition against you with that same constructive resilience that characterized their response to the duplicity of their detractors. Peering beyond the distress of the difficulties assailing them, those heroic souls attempted to translate the Teachings of the new Faith into actions of spiritual and social development. This, too, is your work. Their objective was to build, to strengthen, to refine the tissues of society wherever they might find themselves; and thus, they set up schools, equally educating girls and boys; introduced progressive principles; promoted the sciences; contributed significantly to diverse fields such as agriculture, health, and industry—all of which accrued to the benefit of the nation. You, too, seek to render service to your homeland and to contribute to a renewal of civilization. They responded to the inhumanity of their enemies with patience, calm, resignation, and contentment, choosing to meet deception with truthfulness and cruelty with good will towards all. You, too, demonstrate such noble qualities and, holding fast to these same principles, you belie the slander purveyed against your Faith, evoking the admiration of the fair-minded. (The Universal House of Justice, message dated 9 September 2007, to the Bahá'í students deprived of access to higher education in Iran)

A host of negative forces, generated by the materialism and corruption so widespread in the world, present a challenge in upholding standards of conduct with respect to financial affairs. The members of the younger generation would do well to ponder the difference between gaining wealth through earnest effort in fields such as agriculture, commerce, the arts, and industry, on the one hand, and, on the other, obtaining it without exertion or through dishonourable means. Let them consider the consequences of each for the spiritual development of the individual, as well as the progress of society, and ask themselves what possibilities exist for generating income and acquiring wealth that will ensure true happiness through the development of spiritual qualities, such as honesty, trustworthiness, generosity, justice, and consideration for others, and the recognition that material means are to be expended for the betterment of the world. (The Universal House of Justice, message dated 2 April 2010, to Bahá'ís in the Cradle of the Faith)

COMMUNITY

The fundamental basis of the community is agriculture, tillage of the soil. ('Abdu'l-Bahá, *The Promulgation of Universal Peace*, p. 303)

The solution begins with the village, and when the village is reconstructed, then the cities will be also. ('Abdu'l-Bahá, in *Bahá'í World*, vol. IV, p. 450)

To the far-flung Bahá'í communities of East and West, most of which are being increasingly proscribed and ill treated, and none of which can claim to have had a share of the dual blessings which a specially designed and constructed House of Worship and a fully and efficiently functioning Administrative Order invariably confer, the concentration in a single locality of what will come to be regarded as the fountain-head of the community's spiritual life and what is already recognized as the mainspring of its administrative activities signalizes the launching of yet another phase in the slow and imperceptible emergence, in these declining times, of the model Bahá'í community—a community divinely ordained, organically united, clear-visioned, vibrant with life, and whose very purpose is regulated by the twin directing principles of the worship of God and of service to one's fellow-men. (Shoghi Effendi, handwritten note appended to a letter, dated 4 July 1939, written on his behalf to the National Spiritual Assembly of the United States and Canada, in *Excerpts from The Institution of the Mashriqu'l-Adhkár*. A Statement Prepared by the Research Department of The Universal House of Justice, September 2017)

. . . once a consistent pattern of action is in place, attention needs to be given to extending it more broadly through a network of co-workers and acquaintances, while energies are, at the same time, focused on smaller pockets of the population, each of which should become a centre of intense activity. In an urban cluster, such a centre of activity might best be defined by the boundaries of a neighbourhood; in a cluster that is primarily rural in character, a small village would offer a suitable social space for this purpose. Those who serve in these settings, both local inhabitants and visiting teachers, would rightly view their work in terms of community building. . . . The activities that drive this process, and in which newly found friends are invited to engage—meetings that strengthen the devotional character of the community; classes that nurture the tender hearts and minds of children; groups that channel the surging energies of junior youth; circles of study, open to all, that enable people of varied backgrounds to advance on equal footing and explore the application of the teachings to their individual and collective lives—may well need to be maintained with assistance from outside the local population for a time. It is to be expected, however, that the multiplication of these core activities would soon be sustained by human resources indigenous to the neighbourhood or village itself—by men and women eager to improve material and spiritual conditions in their surroundings. A rhythm of community life should gradually emerge, then, commensurate with the capacity of an expanding nucleus of individuals committed to Bahá'u'lláh's vision of a new World Order. (The Universal House of Justice, Riḍván 2010, to the Bahá'ís of the World)

In every cluster with an intensive programme of growth in operation, efforts need to be made to systematize further the provision of spiritual education to increasing numbers of children, from families of many backgrounds—a requisite of the community-building process gathering momentum in neighbourhoods and villages. (The Universal House of Justice, Riḍván 2010, to the Bahá'ís of the World)

The developments we have mentioned thus far—the rise in capacity to teach the Faith directly and to enter into purposeful discussion on themes of spiritual import with people from every walk of life, the efflorescence of an approach to study of the writings that is wedded to action, the renewal of commitment to provide spiritual education to the young in neighbourhoods and villages on a regular basis, and the spread in influence of a programme that instils in junior youth the sense of a twofold moral purpose, to develop their inherent potentialities and to contribute to the transformation of society—are all reinforced, in no small measure, by yet another advance at the level of culture, the implications of which are far-reaching indeed. This evolution in collective consciousness is discernable in the growing frequency with which the word "accompany" appears in conversations among the friends, a word that is being endowed with new meaning as it is integrated into the common vocabulary of the Bahá'í community. It signals the significant strengthening of a culture in which learning is the mode of operation, a mode that fosters the informed participation of more and more people in a united effort to apply Bahá'u'lláh's teachings to the construction of a divine civilization, which the Guardian states is the primary mission of the Faith. Such an approach offers a striking contrast to the spiritually bankrupt and moribund ways of an old social order that so often seeks to harness human energy through domination, through greed, through guilt or through manipulation. (The Universal House of Justice, Riḍván 2010, to the Bahá'ís of the World)

Bahá'u'lláh's Revelation is vast. It calls for profound change not only at the level of the individual but also in the structure of society. "Is not the object of every Revelation," He Himself proclaims, "to effect a transformation in the whole character of mankind, a transformation that shall manifest itself, both outwardly and inwardly, that shall affect both its inner life and external conditions?" The work advancing in every corner of the globe today represents the latest stage of the ongoing Bahá'í endeavour to create the nucleus of the glorious civilization enshrined in His teachings, the building of which is an enterprise of infinite complexity and scale, one that will demand centuries of exertion by humanity to bring to fruition. There are no shortcuts, no formulas. Only as effort is made to draw on insights from His Revelation, to tap into the accumulating knowledge of the human race, to apply His teachings intelligently to the life of humanity, and to consult on the questions that arise will the necessary learning occur and capacity be developed. (The Universal House of Justice, Riḍván 2010, to the Bahá'ís of the World)

A rich tapestry of community life begins to emerge in every cluster as acts of communal worship, interspersed with discussions undertaken in the intimate setting of the home, are woven together with activities that provide spiritual education to all members of the population—adults, youth and children. Social consciousness is heightened naturally as, for example, lively conversations proliferate among parents regarding the aspirations of their children and service projects spring up at the initiative of junior youth. (The Universal House of Justice, Riḍván 2010, to the Bahá'ís of the World)

. . . as children move seamlessly through the grades year after year and one level of the junior youth spiritual empowerment programme reliably succeeds another. In these places, the training institute is learning to ensure that sufficient human resources are being raised up to provide for the spiritual and moral edification of children and junior youth in ever-increasing numbers. Participation in these foundational activities is becoming so embedded in the culture of the population that it is viewed as an indispensable aspect of the life of a community. A new vitality emerges within a people taking charge of their own development, and they build immunity to those societal forces that breed passivity. Possibilities for material and spiritual progress take shape. Social reality begins to transform. (The Universal House of Justice, Riḍván 2018, to the Bahá'ís of the World)

Furthermore, a House of Worship is to be the spiritual centre of a community and, together with its dependencies that will be created, contributes to a flourishing pattern of collective life. (The Universal House of Justice, letter dated 26 January 2015, to an individual believer, in *The Institution of the Mashriqu'l-Adhkár*. A Statement Prepared by the Research Department of the Universal House of Justice, September 2017)

INSTITUTIONS

First. It is incumbent upon the ministers of the House of Justice to promote the Lesser Peace (Bahá'u'lláh, *Tablets of Bahá'u'lláh*, p. 89)

Bahá'u'lláh says that the Supreme Tribunal must be established: although the League of Nations has been brought into existence, yet it is incapable of establishing universal peace. But the Supreme Tribunal which Bahá'u'lláh has described will fulfil this sacred task with the utmost might and power. ('Abdu'l-Bahá, "First Tablet to The Hague," 17 December 1919, *Pearls of Bounty,* no. 2.1.31)

Today the benefits of universal peace are recognized amongst the people, and likewise the harmful effects of war are clear and manifest to all. But in this matter, knowledge alone is far from sufficient: A power of implementation is needed to establish it throughout the world. ('Abdu'l-Bahá, "Second Tablet to The Hague," 1 July 1920, *Pearls of Bounty,* no. 2.2.6)

In the sacred Laws of God, in every cycle and dispensation, there are blessed feasts, holidays and workless days. On such days all kinds of occupations, commerce, industry, agriculture, etc., are not allowed. . . . As it is a blessed day it should not be neglected or without results by making a day limited to the fruits of mere pleasure. During such blessed days, institutions should be founded that may be of permanent benefit and value to the people so that in current conversation and in history it may become widely known that such a good work was inaugurated on such a feast day. Therefore, the intelligent must search and investigate reality to find out what important affair, what philanthropic institutions are most needed and what foundations should be laid for the community on that particular day, so that they may be established. . . . If, however, the community is in need of widening the circle of commerce or industry or agriculture they should start the means so that the desired aim may be attained. ('Abdu'l-Bahá, in *Social and Economic Development.* A compilation prepared by the Office of Social and Economic Development at the Bahá'í World Center)

The oneness of humanity is, for Bahá'ís, the operating principle and ultimate goal of humankind's collective life on the planet. It is applicable not only to the individual, but also to the relationships that must bind all the states and nations as members of one human family. (Bahá'í International Community, "Conservation and Sustainable Development in the Bahá'í Faith," paper presented by the Bahá'í International Community to the Summit on the Alliance Between Religions and Conservation, 3 May 1995)

Laying the groundwork for global civilization calls for the creation of laws and institutions that are universal in both character and authority. The effort can begin only when the concept of the oneness of humanity has been wholeheartedly embraced by those in whose hands the responsibility for decision making rests, and when the related principles are propagated through both educational systems and the media of mass communication. Once this threshold is crossed, a process will have been set in motion through which the peoples of the world can be drawn into the task of formulating common goals and committing themselves to their attainment. Only so fundamental a reorientation can protect them, too, from the age-old demons of ethnic and religious strife. Only through the dawning consciousness that they constitute a single people will the inhabitants of the planet be enabled to turn away from the patterns of conflict that have dominated social organisation in the past and begin to learn the ways of collaboration and conciliation. "The well-being of mankind," Bahá'u'lláh writes, "its peace and security, are unattainable unless and until its unity is firmly established." (*The Prosperity of Humankind*. A statement prepared by the Bahá'í International Community Office of Public Information, Haifa, 1995)

The second goal centers on institutions: at every level of society, they must serve as channels through which the talents and energies of individuals can be harnessed in service to humanity. Resources that help to develop this individual and institutional capacity represent a true source of wealth to the community. (Bahá'í International Community, "Eradicating Poverty: Moving Forward as One," The Bahá'í International Community's Statement on Poverty, 14 February 2008)

Eliminating hunger and malnutrition; establishing food security; providing adequate shelter; and achieving health for all will require a shift in values, a commitment to equity, and a corresponding re-orientation of policies, goals and programs. Individuals and institutions must work in tandem to take up this task. (Bahá'í International Community, "Eradicating Poverty: Moving Forward as One," The Bahá'í International Community's Statement on Poverty, 14 February 2008)

This question of institutional capacity (e.g. the establishment of regional centers of research and training) constitutes a major challenge to sustainable development. If successfully met, however, the result will be to break the present unbalanced flow of knowledge in the world and dissociate development from ill-conceived processes of modernization. "Modern" technologies will be characterized by an orientation towards addressing locally defined needs and by priorities that take into account both the material and moral prosperity of society as a whole. (Bahá'í International Community, "Rethinking Prosperity: Forging Alternatives to a Culture of Consumerism," Bahá'í International Community's Contribution to the 18th Session of the United Nations Commission on Sustainable Development, 3 May 2010)

We, the undersigned non-governmental organizations in consultative status with the UN Economic and Social Council, leaders of the world's religions and other members of civil society urge the governments of the world to participate in the UN High Level Event on Climate Change through representatives at the highest level and unequivocally call on them to: Consider deeply the ethical and moral questions at the root of the climate change crisis—questions of justice and equity that will determine the survival of cultures, ecosystems, and present as well as future generations; Recognize that the quest for climate justice is not a competition for limited resources but part of an unfolding process towards greater degrees of unity among nations as they endeavor to build a sustainable, just and peaceful civilization. . . . Ensure that commitments in all arenas of the climate change challenge are guided by ethical and moral considerations so as to inspire the trust and confidence of individuals, communities and institutions to effect the changes needed to build a sustainable civilization. We call on the gathered leaders to summon the same spirit and sense of urgency that led to the creation of the United Nations, to forge a climate change agreement worthy of the trust of humankind. (Bahá'í International Community, "Moral and Ethical Dimensions of Climate Change: Appeal to the World's Leaders," September 2009)

Challenging ethical questions of resource distribution and responsibility for damages force governments to develop institutional mechanisms and implement policies that consider the prosperity and health of the global community and that of future generations. . . . At the educational level, curricula must seek to develop a sense of responsibility towards the natural environment as well as foster a spirit of inquiry and innovation so that the diversity of human experience can be brought to bear on the challenge of creating an environmentally sustainable development pathway. (Bahá'í International Community, "Eradicating Poverty: Moving Forward as One," The Bahá'í International Community's Statement on Poverty, 14 February 2008)

The spiritual and administrative centers of the Bahá'í World are by design situated together and surrounded by magnificent beauty. Indeed, it is this design which inspires reflection on the idea that spiritual development, administration of community affairs, and respect for nature are inseparable elements of all programs aimed at promoting the well-being of humanity while building a sustainable world civilization (Bahá'í International Community, "Conservation and Sustainable Development in the Bahá'í Faith," paper presented by the Bahá'í International Community to the Summit on the Alliance between Religions and Conservation, 3 May 1995)

Administration

The friends must engage in the work of developing Persia, that is, they must exert great efforts in the promotion of agriculture, industry, trade, education, arts, and sciences. ('Abdu'l-Bahá, from a Tablet, translated from the Persian, in Universal House of Justice, Research Department, *Agriculture and Rural Life*, 1995)

The intervention of the government and the courts in the problems arising between owners and workers is fully warranted, since these are not such particular matters as are ordinary transactions between two individuals, which do not concern the public and in which the government should have no right to interfere. For problems between owners and workers, though they may appear to be a private matter, are detrimental to the common good, since the commercial, industrial, and agricultural affairs, and even the general business of the nation, are all intimately linked together: An impairment to one is a loss to all. And since the problems between owners and workers are detrimental to the common good, the government and the courts have therefore the right to intervene. ('Abdu'l-Bahá, *Some Answered Questions*, no. 78.10)

To the trustees of the House of Justice He assigns the duty of legislating on matters not expressly provided in His writings, and promised that God will "inspire them with whatsoever He willeth." The establishment of a constitutional form of government, in which the ideals of republicanism and the majesty of kingship, characterized by Him as "one of the signs of God," are combined, He recommends as a meritorious achievement; urges that special regard be paid to the interests of agriculture. (Shoghi Effendi, *God Passes By*, p. 346)

I am much impressed and feel deeply gratified to learn of your devoted and unremitting labors, individually and collectively in the field of service to the Cause; of your constant vigilance and watchful care in upholding its fundamental principles and guarding its essential interests; of the efficiency, faithfulness and vigor with which you are conducting the administration of its affairs throughout that land.

Many and grave may be the obstacles, whether from within or from without, which we shall have to encounter in the days to come, but we feel sure that if we but maintain consistently before our eyes a broad and noble vision of its significance and vital necessity in these days, and above all of its universality and all-conquering power, we shall be enabled to surmount them, one and all, and by the Power of Faith, carry the Ark of the Covenant to its Haven of Safety and Triumph.

It is, I firmly believe, of the utmost urgent importance that, with unity of purpose and action firmly established in our midst, and with every trace of the animosity and mistrust of the past banished from our hearts, we should form one united front and combat, wisely and tactfully, every force that might darken the spirit of the Movement, cause division in its ranks, and narrow it by dogmatic and sectarian belief.

It is primarily upon the elected members of the National Spiritual Assemblies throughout the Bahá'í world that this highly important duty devolves, as in their hands the direction and management of all spiritual Bahá'í activities have been placed and centralized, and as they constitute in the eyes of the people of their country the supreme body in that land that officially represents, promotes and safeguards the various interests of the Cause, it is my fervent prayer and my most cherished desire, that the unfailing guidance of Bahá'u'lláh and the blessings of our beloved Master will enable them to set a high and true example to all other Bahá'í institutions and local Assemblies, and will show them what absolute harmony, mature deliberation and whole-hearted cooperation can achieve. (Shoghi Effendi, message dated 9 April 1923, to the members of the American National Spiritual Assembly, *Bahá'í Administration,* pp. 45–48)

The responsibilities of the members of the Spiritual Assemblies that are engaged in teaching the Cause of God in Eastern lands have been clearly laid down in the holy Texts. These bid them to work towards the improvement of morals and the spread of learning; to strive to eradicate ignorance and unenlightenment, eliminate prejudice, and reinforce the foundation of true faith in people's hearts and minds; to seek to develop self-reliance and avoidance of blind imitation; to aim to enhance the efficient management of their affairs, and observe purity and refinement in all circumstances; to show their commitment to truthfulness and honesty, and their ability to conduct themselves with frankness, courage and resolution. They similarly enjoin them to lend their support to agricultural and industrial development, to consolidate the foundations of mutual assistance and co-operation, to promote the emancipation and advancement of women and support the compulsory education of both sexes, to encourage application of the principles of consultation among all classes, and to adhere in all dealings to a standard of scrupulous integrity. (Shoghi Effendi, message dated 30 January 1926, to the Spiritual Assemblies throughout the East, in Universal House of Justice, Research Department, *Agriculture and Rural Life*, 1995)

Bahá'í administration has no aim except the good of all nations and it does not take any steps that are against the public good. Contrary to the conception the word "administration" may create in the mind because of the similarity in name, it does not resemble the current organizations of political parties; it does not interfere in political affairs; and it is the safeguard against the involvement of Bahá'ís in subversive political activities. Its high ideals are "to improve the characters of men; to extend the scope of knowledge; to abolish ignorance and prejudice; to strengthen the foundations of true religion in all hearts; to encourage self-reliance and discourage false imitation; . . . to uphold truthfulness, audacity, frankness, and courage; to promote craftsmanship and agriculture; . . . to educate, on a compulsory basis, children of both sexes; to insist on integrity in business transactions; to lay stress on the observance of honesty and piety; . . . to acquire mastery and skill in the modern sciences and arts; to promote the interests of the public; . . . to obey outwardly and inwardly and with true loyalty the regulations enacted by state and government; . . . to honor, to extol and to follow the example of those who have distinguished themselves in science and learning."

And again, ". . . to help the needy from every creed or sect, and to collaborate with the people of the country in all welfare services."

In brief, whatever the clergy in other religions undertake individually and by virtue of their appointment to their positions, the Bahá'í administration performs collectively and through an elective process. (The Universal House of Justice, message dated 19 October 1983, to all National Spiritual Assemblies)

As to your worry about over-controlling the friends: by appreciating the nature of the power of action which they possess, you will be able to gauge how best to guide and direct them. A wide latitude for action must be allowed them, which means that a large margin for mistakes must also be allowed. Your National Assembly and the Local Assemblies must not react automatically to every mistake, but distinguish between those that are self-correcting with the passage of time and do no particular harm to the community and those which require Assembly intervention. Related to this is the tendency of the friends to criticize each other at the slightest provocation, whereas the Teachings call upon them to encourage each other. Such tendencies are of course motivated by a deep love for the Faith, a desire to see it free of any flaw. But human beings are not perfect. The Local Assemblies and the friends must be helped through your example and through loving counsel to refrain from such a pattern of criticism, which stunts the growth and development of the community. You should also be fearful of laying down too many rules and regulations. The Cause is not so fragile that a degree of mistakes cannot be tolerated. When you feel that certain actions may become trends with harmful consequences, you may, instead of making a new rule, discuss the matter with the Counselors, enlisting their support in educating the friends in a manner that will improve their understanding and their conduct. (The Universal House of Justice, letter dated

19 May 1994, to The National Spiritual Assembly of the Bahá'ís of the United States)

The oneness of humanity, which is the primary principle and ultimate goal of the Cause of Bahá'u'lláh, implies, as Shoghi Effendi said, an "organic change in the structure of present-day society." So fundamental a change in the structural conception of society must also imply a new pattern for the administration of community affairs in a Bahá'í context. . . . The friends must never mistake the Bahá'í administration for an end in itself. It is merely the instrument of the spirit of the Faith. This Cause is a Cause which God has revealed to humanity as a whole. It is designed to benefit the entire human race, and the only way it can do this is to reform the community life of mankind, as well as seeking to regenerate the individual. The Bahá'í Administration is only the first shaping of what in future will come to be the social life and laws of community living. (The Universal House of Justice, letter dated 19 May 1994, to The National Spiritual Assembly of the Bahá'ís of the United States)

In the Tablet of the World Bahá'u'lláh states that "Everyone, whether man or woman, should hand over to a trusted person a portion of what he or she earneth through trade, agriculture or other occupation, for the training and education of children, to be spent for this purpose with the knowledge of the Trustees of the House of Justice." In many countries this duty is fulfilled through the taxes that the government levies for the support of the state educational system, but there are other lands where no such facilities are provided and the Local Spiritual Assemblies may well begin to fulfill this aspect of their duties by encouraging the local friends to contribute to a special education fund which can be used for the support of tutorial schools or to assist the children of indigent believers to obtain schooling.

(The Universal House of Justice, Naw-Rúz 1979, to all National Spiritual Assemblies)

The growing maturity of a world-wide religious community, which all these processes indicate is further evidenced in the reaching out, by a number of national communities to the social and economic life of their countries, exemplified by the founding of tutorial schools, the inception of radio stations, the pursuit of rural development programs and the operation of medical and agricultural schemes. (The Universal House of Justice, Riḍván 1983, to the Bahá'ís of the World)

The institutions of the Administrative Order of Bahá'u'lláh, rooted in the provisions of His Revelation, have emerged gradually and organically, as the Bahá'í community has grown through the power of the divine impulse imparted to humankind in this age. The characteristics and functions of each of these institutions have evolved, and are still evolving, as are the relationships between them. (The Universal House of Justice, message dated 30 May 1997, to all National Spiritual Assemblies)

Progress in the development field will largely depend on natural stirrings at the grass roots, and it should receive its driving force from those sources rather than from an imposition of plans and programs from the top. The major task of National Assemblies, therefore, is to increase the local communities' awareness of needs and possibilities, and to guide and coordinate the efforts resulting from such awareness. (The Universal House of Justice, message dated 20 October 1983, to the Bahá'ís of the World)

There are spiritual principles, or what some call human values, by which solutions can be found for every social problem. Any well-intentioned group can in a general sense devise practical solutions to its problems, but good intentions and practical knowledge are usually not enough. The essential merit of spiritual principle is that it not only presents a perspective which harmonizes with that which is immanent in human nature, it also induces an attitude, a dynamic, a will, an aspiration, which facilitate the discovery and implementation of practical measures. Leaders of governments and all in authority would be well served in their efforts to solve problems if they would first seek to identify the principles involved and then be guided by them. (The Universal House of Justice, *The Promise of World Peace*, 1985, To the Peoples of the World)

The Local Spiritual Assemblies of such villages must gradually widen the scope of their activities, not only to develop every aspect of the spiritual life of the believers within their jurisdiction, but also, through Bahá'í consultation and through such principles as harmony between science and religion, the importance of education, and work as a form of worship, to promote the standards of agriculture and other skills in the life of the people. (From a letter written on behalf of the Universal House of Justice, dated 27 July 1976, to an individual believer, in Universal House of Justice, Research Department, *Agriculture and Rural Life*, 1995)

The mode of operation adopted in the area of social and economic development, in common with other areas of Bahá'í activity, is one of learning in action. When efforts are carried out in a learning mode—characterized by constant action, reflection, consultation, and study—visions and strategies are re-examined time and again. As tasks are accomplished, obstacles removed, resources multiplied, and lessons learned, modifications are made in goals and methods. The learning process, which is given direction through appropriate institutional arrangements, unfolds in a way that resembles the growth and differentiation of a living organism. Haphazard change is avoided, and continuity of action maintained. (*Social Action*. A paper prepared by the Office of Social and Economic Development at the Bahá'í World Center, 26 November 2012)

Mashriqu'l–Adhkár
Build ye houses of worship throughout the lands in the name of Him Who is the Lord of all religions. (Bahá'u'lláh, The Kitáb-i-Aqdas, ¶31)

Say: The Mashriqu'l-Adhkár is each and every building which hath been erected in cities and villages for the celebration of My praise. Such is the name by which it hath been designated before the throne of glory, were ye of those who understand. (Bahá'u'lláh, The Kitáb-i-Aqdas, ¶115)

The Mashriqu'l-Adhkár is one of the most vital institutions in the world, and it hath many subsidiary branches. Although it is a House of Worship, it is also connected with a hospital, a drug dispensary, a traveler's hospice, a school for orphans, and a university for advanced studies. Every Mashriqu'l-Adhkár is connected with these five things. ('Abdu'l-Bahá, *Selections from the Writings of 'Abdu'l-Bahá*, no. 64.1)

Regarding what ye had written as to the Mashriqu'l-Adhkár's having been established in the Land of Ṭá and that, by the grace of God, it hath been and is being instituted in other places: this matter was mentioned in His Holy and Most Exalted Presence, whereupon the tongue of the Ancient of Days made answer: "Blessed is the spot, and the house, and the place, and the city, and the heart, and the mountain, and the refuge, and the cave, and the valley, and the land, and the sea, and the island, and the meadow where mention of God hath been made, and His praise glorified." ('Abdu'l-Bahá, from a Tablet—translated from the Arabic and Persian, quoted in *The Institution of the Mashriqu'l-Adhkár*. A Statement Prepared by the Research Department of The Universal House of Justice, September 2017)

And of all the institutions that stand associated with His Holy Name, surely none save the institution of the Mashriqu'l-Adhkár can most adequately provide the essentials of Bahá'í worship and service, both so vital to the regeneration of the world. (Shoghi Effendi, letter dated October 25, 1929, *Bahá'í Administration,* p. 186)

Nothing short of direct and constant interaction between the spiritual forces emanating from this House of Worship centering in the heart of the Mashriqu'l-Adhkár, and the energies consciously displayed by those who administer its affairs in their service to humanity can possibly provide the necessary agency capable of removing the ills that have so long and so grievously afflicted humanity. (Shoghi Effendi, letter dated October 25, 1929, *Bahá'í Administration,* p. 186)

It should be borne in mind that the central Edifice of the Mashriqu'l-Adhkár, round which in the fullness of time shall cluster such institutions of social service shall afford relief to the suffering, sustenance to the poor, shelter to the wayfarer, solace to the bereaved, and education to the ignorant, should be regarded apart from these Dependencies, as a House solely designed and entirely dedicated to the worship of God in accordance with the few yet definitely prescribed principles established by Bahá'u'lláh in the Kitáb-i-Aqdas. (Shoghi Effendi, letter dated October 25, 1929, *Bahá'í Administration*, p. 184)

The oneness of mankind, which is at once the operating principle and ultimate goal of His Revelation, implies the achievement of a dynamic coherence between the spiritual and practical requirements of life on earth. The indispensability of this coherence is unmistakably illustrated in His ordination of the Mashriqu'l-Adhkár, the spiritual center of every Bahá'í community round which must flourish dependencies dedicated to the social, humanitarian, educational and scientific advancement of mankind. (The Universal House of Justice, message dated 20 October 1983, to the Bahá'ís of the World)

These dependencies—centres of education and scientific learning as well as cultural and humanitarian endeavour—embody the ideals of social and spiritual progress to be achieved through the application of knowledge, and demonstrate how, when religion and science are in harmony, they elevate the station of the human being and lead to the flourishing of civilization. (The Universal House of Justice, message dated 18 December 2014, to the Bahá'ís in Iran)

CONSULTATION

Languages must be reduced to one common language to be taught in all the schools of the world. (Bahá'u'lláh, *Tablets of Bahá'u'lláh*, p. 89)

The day is approaching when all the peoples of the world will have adopted one universal language and one common script. When this is achieved, to whatsoever city a man may journey, it shall be as if he were entering his own home. These things are obligatory and absolutely essential. It is incumbent upon every man of insight and understanding to strive to translate that which hath been written into reality and action. (Bahá'u'lláh, *Tablets of Bahá'u'lláh*, p. 11)

The Great Being saith: The heaven of divine wisdom is illumined with the two luminaries of consultation and compassion. Take ye counsel together in all matters, inasmuch as consultation is the lamp of guidance which leadeth the way, and is the bestower of understanding. (Bahá'u'lláh, *Tablets of Bahá'u'lláh*, p. 168)

O ye the elected representatives of the people in every land! Take ye counsel together, and let your concern be only for that which profiteth mankind and bettereth the condition thereof, if ye be of them that scan heedfully. Regard the world as the human body which, though at its creation whole and perfect, hath been afflicted, through various causes, with grave disorders and maladies. Not for one day did it gain ease, nay its sickness waxed more severe, as it fell under the treatment of ignorant physicians, who gave full rein to their personal desires and have erred grievously. And if, at one time, through the care of an able physician, a member of that body was healed, the rest remained afflicted as before. Thus informeth you the All-Knowing, the All-Wise. (Bahá'u'lláh, *The Summons of the Lord of Hosts*, no. 1.174)

Say: no man can attain his true station except through his justice. No power can exist except through unity. No welfare and no well-being can be attained except through consultation. (Bahá'u'lláh, from a Tablet translated from the Arabic, in *Consultation: A Compilation Prepared by the Research Department of the Universal House of Justice*)

The question of consultation is of the utmost importance, and is one of the most potent instruments conducive to the tranquillity and felicity of the people. For example, when a believer is uncertain about his affairs, or when he seeketh to pursue a project or trade, the friends should gather together and devise a solution for him. He, in his turn, should act accordingly. ('Abdu'l-Bahá, from a Tablet— translated from the Persian, in *Consultation: A Compilation Prepared by the Research Department of The Universal House of Justice*)

The prime requisites for them that take counsel together are purity of motive, radiance of spirit, detachment from all else save God, attraction to His Divine Fragrances, humility and lowliness amongst His loved ones, patience and long-suffering in difficulties and servitude to His exalted Threshold. Should they be graciously aided to acquire these attributes, victory from the unseen Kingdom of Bahá shall be vouchsafed to them. ('Abdu'l-Bahá, *Selections from the Writings of 'Abdu'l-Bahá*, no. 43.1)

For instance, when a man hath a project to accomplish, should he consult with some of his brethren, that which is agreeable will of course be investigated and unveiled to his eyes, and the truth will be disclosed. Likewise on a higher level, should the people of a village consult one another about their affairs, the right solution will certainly be revealed. In like manner, the members of each profession, such as in industry, should consult, and those in commerce should similarly consult on business affairs. In short, consultation is desirable and acceptable in all things and on all issues. (Shoghi Effendi, letter dated 15 February 1922, to the National Spiritual Assembly of Persia)

Let us also bear in mind that the keynote of the Cause of God is not dictatorial authority, but humble fellowship, not arbitrary power, but the spirit of frank and loving consultation. Nothing short of the spirit of a true Bahá'í can hope to reconcile the principles of mercy and justice, of freedom and submission, of the sanctity of the right of the individual and of self-surrender, of vigilance, discretion and prudence on the one hand and fellowship, candour and courage on the other. (Shoghi Effendi, letter dated 23 February 1924, to the Bahá'ís of America, *Bahá'í Administration*, p. 63)

Bahá'u'lláh enjoins the adoption of a universal language and script. His Writings envisage two stages in this process. The first stage is to consist of the selection of an existing language or an invented one which would then be taught in all the schools of the world as an auxiliary to the mother tongues. The governments of the world through their parliaments are called upon to effect this momentous enactment. The second stage, in the distant future, would be the eventual adoption of one single language and common script for all on earth. (The Universal House of Justice, *The Kitáb-i-Aqdas*, Notes, no. 193)

Bahá'u'lláh has established consultation as one of the fundamental principles of His Faith and has exhorted the believers to *"take counsel together in all matters."* He describes consultation as *"the lamp of guidance which leadeth the way"* and as *"the bestower of understanding."* Shoghi Effendi states that the "principle of consultation . . . constitutes one of the basic laws" of the Bahá'í Administrative Order. (The Universal House of Justice, *The Kitáb-i-Aqdas*, Notes, no. 52)

Bahá'u'lláh insistently drew attention to the virtues and indispensability of consultation for ordering human affairs. He said: "Consultation bestows greater awareness and transmutes conjecture into certitude. It is a shining light which, in a dark world, leads the way and guides. For everything there is and will continue to be a station of perfection and maturity. The maturity of the gift of understanding is made manifest through consultation." The very attempt to achieve peace through the consultative action he proposed can release such a salutary spirit among the peoples of the earth that no power could resist the final, triumphal outcome. (The Universal House of Justice, *The Promise of World Peace*, 1985, To the Peoples of the World)

Develop the proper understanding and practice of consultation among members of the Bahá'í community and in the work of Bahá'í institutions, and foster the spirit of consultation in the conduct of human affairs and the resolution of conflicts at all levels of society. (The Universal House of Justice, message dated 25 February 1986, to all National Spiritual Assemblies)

It is important to realize that the spirit of Bahá'í consultation is very different from that current in the decision-making processes of non-Bahá'í bodies.

The ideal of Bahá'í consultation is to arrive at a unanimous decision. When this is not possible a vote must be taken. In the words of the beloved Guardian: ". . . when they are called upon to arrive at a certain decision, they should, after dispassionate, anxious, and cordial consultation, turn to God in prayer, and with earnestness and conviction and courage record their vote and abide by the voice of the majority, which we are told by our Master to be the voice of truth, never to be challenged, and always to be wholeheartedly enforced."

As soon as a decision is reached it becomes the decision of the whole Assembly, not merely of those members who happened to be among the majority.

When it is proposed to put a matter to the vote, a member of the Assembly may feel that there are additional facts or views which must be sought before he can make up his mind and intelligently vote on the proposition. He should express this feeling to the Assembly, and it is for the Assembly to decide whether or not further consultation is needed before voting. (The Universal House of Justice, letter dated 6 March 1970, to the National Spiritual Assembly of the Bahá'ís of Canada)

The outstanding development in the relationship of the Bahá'í International Community to the United Nations was the accreditation of that Community as a nongovernmental organization with consultative status to the Economic and Social Council of the United Nations. The Bahá'í International Community now has a permanent representative at the United Nations and maintains an office in New York. (The Universal House of Justice, Riḍván 1973, to the Bahá'ís of the World)

More than a century ago, 'Abdu'l-Bahá referred to "unity of thought in world undertakings, the consummation of which will erelong be witnessed." The recently adopted international agreement on climate change, irrespective of any shortcomings and limitations it may have, offers another noteworthy demonstration of that development anticipated by 'Abdu'l-Bahá. The agreement represents a starting point for constructive thought and action that can be refined or revised on the basis of experience and new findings over time. (From a letter written on behalf of the Universal House of Justice, dated 29 November 2017, to three individuals)

In those parts of the world where discussions surrounding anthropogenic climate change have indeed fallen prey to an almost intractable divide, Bahá'ís must be sensitive to the danger of this divisive partisan approach taking root in the community. This may well mean that some individuals or agencies have to consider to what extent their views about action required on climate change reflect a posture that is too extreme, whether in exaggerating the problem or minimizing it. Concepts and principles associated with Bahá'í consultation inform how the friends should interact among themselves and how they participate in social discourses and social action. Consultation provides a means by which common understanding can be reached and a collective course of action defined. It involves a free, respectful, dignified, and fair-minded effort on the part of a group of people to exchange views, seek truth, and attempt to reach consensus. An initial difference of opinion is the starting point for examining an issue in order to reach greater understanding and consensus; it should not become a cause of rancor, aversion, or estrangement. By acting in unity, a conclusion about a particular course of action may be tested and revised as necessary through a process of learning. Otherwise, as 'Abdu'l-Bahá explains, "stubbornness and persistence in one's views will lead ultimately to discord and wrangling and the truth will remain hidden." (From a letter written on behalf of the Universal House of Justice, dated 29 November 2017, to three individuals)

Central to the capacity of a Bahá'í community to lead a process of transformation is the ability of its members and institutions to apply the Revelation of Bahá'u'lláh to various aspects of life and thereby establish consistent patterns of change. . . . The believers must regularly engage in consultation, action, reflection—all in the light of the guidance inherent in the Teachings of the Faith. *(Bahá'í Social and Economic Development: Prospects for the Future,* 16 September 1993. A statement approved by the Universal House of Justice for use in orienting and guiding the work of Bahá'í social and economic development throughout the world)

If learning in action is to be the primary mode of operation in the area of social and economic development, the Bahá'í principle of consultation needs to be fully appreciated. Whether concerned with analysing a specific problem, attaining higher degrees of understanding on a given issue, or exploring possible courses of action, consultation may be seen as collective search for truth. Participants in a consultative process see reality from different points of view, and as these views are examined and understood, clarity is achieved. In this conception of the collective investigation of reality, truth is not a compromise between opposing interest groups. Nor does the desire to exercise power over one another animate participants in the consultative process. What they seek, rather, is the power of unified thought and action. (*Social Action*. A paper prepared by the Office of Social and Economic Development at the Bahá'í World Center, 26 November 2012)

Central to the task of reconceptualizing the system of human relationships is the process that Bahá'u'lláh refers to as consultation. "In all things it is necessary to consult," is His advice. "The maturity of the gift of understanding is made manifest through consultation." (*The Prosperity of Humankind*. A statement prepared by the Bahá'í International Community Office of Public Information, Haifa, 1995)

At the group level, a concern for justice is the indispensable compass in collective decision making, because it is the only means by which unity of thought and action can be achieved. Far from encouraging the punitive spirit that has often masqueraded under its name in past ages, justice is the practical expression of awareness that, in the achievement of human progress, the interests of the individual and those of society are inextricably linked. To the extent that justice becomes a guiding concern of human interaction, a consultative climate is encouraged that permits options to be examined dispassionately and appropriate courses of action selected. In such a climate the perennial tendencies toward manipulation and partisanship are far less likely to deflect the decision-making process. (*The Prosperity of Humankind*. A statement prepared by the Bahá'í International Community Office of Public Information, Haifa, 1995)

Consultation must replace confrontation and domination in order to gain the cooperation of the family of nations in devising and implementing measures that will preserve the earth's ecological balance. (Bahá'í International Community, *Earth Charter*, 5 April 1991. The statement offering suggestions for the proposed "Earth Charter," was originally presented by the Bahá'í International Community to the Preparatory Committee of the United Nations Conference on Environment and Development (UNCED), June 1992)

It is our conviction that any call to global action for environment and development must be rooted in universally accepted values and principles. Similarly, the search for solutions to the world's grave environmental and developmental problems must go beyond technical-utilitarian proposals and address the underlying causes of the crisis. Genuine solutions, in the Bahá'í view, will require a globally accepted vision for the future, based on unity and willing cooperation among the nations, races, creeds, and classes of the human family. Commitment to a higher moral standard, equality between the sexes, and the development of consultative skills for the effective functioning of groups at all levels of society will be essential. (Bahá'í International Community, *Earth Charter*, 5 April 1991. The statement offering suggestions for the proposed "Earth Charter," was originally presented by the Bahá'í International Community to the Preparatory Committee of the United Nations Conference on Environment and Development (UNCED), June 1992)

The Bahá'í world will intensify the process of seeking to apply spiritual principles of unity, justice, solidarity and moderation to the economic, technological, social and political challenges of today. It will increasingly collaborate with like-minded individuals and groups— including organizations of civil society, government and others—to help bring about the fundamental changes needed in society if peace and sustainable development are to be realized. (Bahá'í International Community, "Conservation and Sustainable Development in the Bahá'í Faith," paper presented by the Bahá'í International Community to the Summit on the Alliance Between Religions and Conservation, 3 May 1995)

Top-down models of community development can no longer adequately respond to modern day needs and aspirations. The world community must move toward more participatory, knowledge-based and values-driven systems of governance in which people can assume responsibility for the processes and institutions that affect their lives. These systems need to be democratic in spirit and method, and must emerge on all levels of world society, including the global level. Consultation—the expression of justice in human affairs— should become their primary mode of decision-making. (Bahá'í International Community, "Statement on Sustainable Communities in an Integrating World," 1996)

DISCOURSE AND SOCIAL ACTION

This servant appealeth to every diligent and enterprising soul to exert his utmost endeavor and arise to rehabilitate the conditions in all regions and to quicken the dead with the living waters of wisdom and utterance, by virtue of the love he cherisheth for God, the One, the Peerless, the Almighty, the Beneficent. (Bahá'u'lláh, *Tablets of Bahá'u'lláh*, p. 11)

Purge thou thy heart that We may cause fountains of wisdom and utterance to gush out therefrom, thus enabling thee to raise thy voice among all mankind. Unloose thy tongue and proclaim the truth for the sake of the remembrance of thy merciful Lord. Be not afraid of anyone, place thy whole trust in God, the Almighty, the All-Knowing. (Bahá'u'lláh, *Tablets of Bahá'u'lláh*, p. 12)

Every word is endowed with a spirit, therefore the speaker or ex-pounder should carefully deliver his words at the appropriate time and place, for the impression which each word maketh is clearly evident and perceptible. The Great Being saith: One word may be likened unto fire, another unto light, and the influence which both exert is manifest in the world. Therefore an enlightened man of wis-dom should primarily speak with words as mild as milk, that the children of men may be nurtured and edified thereby and may attain the ultimate goal of human existence which is the station of true understanding and nobility. And likewise He saith: One word is like unto springtime causing the tender saplings of the rose-garden of knowledge to become verdant and flourishing, while another word is even as a deadly poison. It behooveth a prudent man of wisdom to speak with utmost leniency and forbearance so that the sweetness of his words may induce everyone to attain that which befitteth man's station. (Bahá'u'lláh, *Tablets of Bahá'u'lláh*, p. 11)

O Son of Dust! The wise are they that speak not unless they obtain a hearing, even as the cup-bearer, who proffereth not his cup till he findeth a seeker, and the lover who crieth not out from the depths of his heart until he gazeth upon the beauty of his beloved. Wherefore sow the seeds of wisdom and knowledge in the pure soil of the heart, and keep them hidden, till the hyacinths of divine wisdom spring from the heart and not from mire and clay. (Bahá'u'lláh, The Hidden Words, Persian, no. 36)

How manifold are the truths which must remain unuttered until the appointed time is come! Even as it hath been said: "Not everything that a man knoweth can be disclosed, nor can everything that he can disclose be regarded as timely, nor can every timely utterance be considered as suited to the capacity of those who hear it." (Bahá'u'lláh, *Gleanings from the Writings of Bahá'u'lláh*, no. 89.3)

Follow thou the way of thy Lord, and say not that which the ears cannot bear to hear, for such speech is like luscious food given to small children. However palatable, rare and rich the food may be, it cannot be assimilated by the digestive organs of a suckling child. Therefore unto every one who hath a right, let his settled measure be given.

"Not everything that a man knoweth can be disclosed, nor can everything that he can disclose be regarded as timely, nor can every timely utterance be considered as suited to the capacity of those who hear it." Such is the consummate wisdom to be observed in thy pursuits. Be not oblivious thereof, if thou wishest to be a man of action under all conditions. First diagnose the disease and identify the malady, then prescribe the remedy, for such is the perfect method of the skillful physician. ('Abdu'l-Bahá, *Selections from the Writings of 'Abdu'l-Bahá,* no. 214.1–2)

In this day, however, means of communication have multiplied, and the five continents of the earth have virtually merged into one. And for everyone it is now easy to travel to any land, to associate and exchange views with its peoples, and to become familiar, through publications, with the conditions, the religious beliefs and the thoughts of all men. ('Abdu'l-Bahá, *Selections from the Writings of 'Abdu'l-Bahá*, no. 15.6)

. . . [Bahá'u'lláh] urges that special regard be paid to the interests of agriculture; and makes specific reference to "the swiftly appearing newspapers," describes them as "the mirror of the world" and as "an amazing and potent phenomenon," and prescribes to all who are responsible for their production the duty to be sanctified from malice, passion and prejudice, to be just and fair-minded, to be painstaking in their inquiries, and ascertain all the facts in every situation. (Shoghi Effendi, *God Passes By*, p. 346)

This Bahá'í teaching of human fellowship and kindness implies that we must be always ready to extend every assistance and help we can to those who are in distress and suffering. Bahá'í charity is of the very essence of the Teachings, and should therefore be developed in every Bahá'í community. Charitable institutions, such as orphanages, free schools and hospitals for the poor, constitute an indispensable part of the Mashriqu'l-Adhkár. It is the responsibility of every local Bahá'í community to ensure the welfare of its poor and needy members, through whatever means possible. (Shoghi Effendi, letter dated 26 June 1936, to an individual believer, in *The Institution of the Mashriqu'l-Adhkár*. A Statement Prepared by the Research Department of the Universal House of Justice, September 2017)

Bahá'í contributions to discourses newly prevalent in society are generating heightened interest, and there is a responsibility to be discharged here too. At a time when the urgency of attaining higher levels of unity, founded on the incontestable truth of humanity's oneness, is becoming apparent to larger and larger numbers, society stands in need of clear voices that can articulate the spiritual principles that underlie such an aspiration. (The Universal House of Justice, letter dated 9 May 2020, to all National Spiritual Assemblies)

Central to the effort to advance the work of expansion and consolidation, social action, and the involvement in the discourses of society is the notion of an evolving conceptual framework, a matrix that organizes thought and gives shape to activities and which becomes more elaborate as experience accumulates. (The Universal House of Justice, letter dated 24 July 2013, to the National Spiritual Assembly of the Bahá'ís of Canada)

Closely related to the habit of reducing an entire theme into one or two appealing phrases is the tendency to perceive dichotomies, where, in fact, there are none. It is essential that ideas forming part of a cohesive whole not be held in opposition to one another. In a letter written on his behalf, Shoghi Effendi warned: "We must take the teachings as a great, balanced whole, not seek out and oppose to each other two strong statements that have different meanings; somewhere in between, there are links uniting the two." (The Universal House of Justice, message dated 28 December 2010, to the Conference of the Continental Boards of Counsellors)

The Faith's standing in various spaces in which discourses unfold has been much enhanced by its official presence on the World Wide Web, a presence which has expanded considerably through the launch of numerous national Bahá'í websites and the further development of the family of sites associated with Bahai.org. (The Universal House of Justice, Riḍván 2018, to the Bahá'ís of the World)

As the work of community building intensifies, the friends are using the new capacities they have developed to improve conditions in the society around them, their enthusiasm kindled by their study of the divine teachings. Short-term projects have soared in number, formal programmes have expanded their reach, and there are now more Bahá'í-inspired development organizations engaged in education, health, agriculture, and other areas. From the resulting transformation visible in the individual and collective lives of peoples may be discerned the unmistakable stirrings of the society-building power of the Cause of Bahá'u'lláh. No wonder, then, that it is from such instances of social action—whether simple or complex, of fixed duration or long sustained—that the Offices of the Bahá'í International Community are increasingly taking inspiration in their efforts to participate in the prevalent discourses of society. . . . And wherever they live, work, or study, believers of all ages and backgrounds are making valued contributions to particular discourses, bringing to the attention of those around them a principled perspective shaped by Bahá'u'lláh's vast Revelation. (The Universal House of Justice, Riḍván 2018, to the Bahá'ís of the World)

They are called upon to become increasingly involved in the life of society, benefiting from its educational programmes, excelling in its trades and professions, learning to employ well its tools, and applying themselves to the advancement of its arts and sciences. At the same time, they are never to lose sight of the aim of the Faith to effect a transformation of society, remoulding its institutions and processes, on a scale never before witnessed. To this end, they must remain acutely aware of the inadequacies of current modes of thinking and doing—this, without feeling the least degree of superiority, without assuming an air of secrecy or aloofness, and without adopting an unnecessarily critical stance towards society. (The Universal

73

House of Justice, message dated 28 December 2010, to the Conference of the Continental Board of Counsellors)

Effective social action serves to enrich participation in the discourses of society, just as the insights gained from engaging in certain discourses can help to clarify the concepts that shape social action. At the level of the cluster, involvement in public discourse can range from an act as simple as introducing Bahá'í ideas into everyday conversation to more formal activities such as the preparation of articles and attendance at gatherings, dedicated to themes of social concern—climate change and the environment, governance and human rights, to mention a few. It entails, as well, meaningful interactions with civic groups and local organizations in villages and neighbourhoods. (The Universal House of Justice, Riḍván 2010, to the Bahá'ís of the World)

The expectation we expressed in our Naw-Rúz message that this test of humanity's endurance would grant it greater insight is already being realized. Leaders, prominent thinkers, and commentators have begun to explore fundamental concepts and bold aspirations that, in recent times, have been largely absent from public discourse. At present these are but early glimmerings, yet they hold out the possibility that a moment of collective consciousness may be in view. (The Universal House of Justice, Riḍván 2020, to the Bahá'ís of the World)

And wherever they live, work, or study, believers of all ages and backgrounds are making valued contributions to particular discourses, bringing to the attention of those around them a principled perspective shaped by Bahá'u'lláh's vast Revelation. (The Universal House of Justice, Riḍván 2018, to the Bahá'ís of the World)

Progress in the development field will largely depend on natural stir-rings at the grass roots, and it should receive its driving force from those sources rather than from an imposition of plans and programs from the top. The major task of National Assemblies, therefore, is to increase the local communities' awareness of needs and possibilities, and to guide and coordinate the efforts resulting from such aware-ness. (The Universal House of Justice, message dated 20 October 1983, to the Bahá'ís of the World)

Even though individuals may strive to be guided in their actions by their personal understanding of the Divine Texts, and much can be accomplished thereby, such actions, untempered by the overall direction provided by authorized institutions, are incapable of at-taining the thrust necessary for the unencumbered advancement of civilization. (The Universal House of Justice, message dated 19 May 1994, to The National Spiritual Assembly of the Bahá'ís of the Unit-ed States)

Bahá'í activity in the field of social and economic development seeks to promote the well-being of people of all walks of life, whatever their beliefs or background. It represents the efforts of the Bahá'í community to effect constructive social change, as it learns to apply the teachings of the Faith, together with knowledge accumulated in different fields of human endeavour, to social reality. Its purpose is neither to proclaim the Cause nor to serve as a vehicle for conver-sion. (The Universal House of Justice, *Social Action*, 26 November, 2012, to all National Spiritual Assemblies)

Already in many areas the friends are witnessing the confirmations of their initiatives in such pursuits as the founding of tutorial and other schools, the promotion of literacy, the launching of rural development programs, the inception of educational radio stations, and the operation of agricultural and medical projects. (The Universal House of Justice, message dated 20 October 1983, to the Bahá'ís of the World)

When the Bahá'í community grows sufficiently large, however, its activities can and must proliferate and diversify. This development is already taking place in many parts of the world. In India, for example, the New Era School in Panchgani, which has been developing remarkably for a number of years, is closely associated with a rural development project in the villages close by that is having dramatically favorable results in the life of the villagers. In the province of Madhya Pradesh, where there are hundreds of thousands of Bahá'ís, the Rabbani School in Gwalior is educating children from the villages of the area in the Teachings of the Faith, in academic subjects and in agriculture, so that when they return to their home villages, these pupils not only promote the Faith but will influence their growth and development in every way. (The Universal House of Justice, Riḍván 1983, to the Bahá'ís of the World)

Two emerging realities have prompted us to address these words to you. The first reality is the growing consciousness around the world of the looming and appalling dangers carried by the coronavirus pandemic. In many countries, despite valiant and determined collective efforts to avert disaster, the situation is already grave, creating tragedies for families and individuals and plunging whole societies into crisis. Waves of suffering and sorrow are breaking over one place after another, and will weaken different nations, at different moments, in different ways.

The second reality, one that is daily more apparent, is the resilience and undiminished vitality of the Bahá'í world in the face of a challenge which has no likeness in living memory. . . . Learning from the experience gained in other parts of the world, some communities have found safe and creative ways to raise awareness of public health requirements within populations. Special attention is being paid to those who are most at risk from the virus and the economic hardship arising from its spread; the initiatives featured on the Bahá'í World News Service in this regard are but a mere handful of the countless number under way. These are being complemented by efforts to examine, promote, and cultivate those spiritual qualities which are most needed at this time. Many such efforts are necessarily taking place in family units or in solitude, but where conditions allow or communication tools make it possible, a sense of extraordinary solidarity is being actively nurtured among souls sharing similar circumstances. The dynamics of community life, so important for collective progress, will not be subdued. . . . The comfort we take at seeing the resilience of the Bahá'í world manifest itself in action is tempered by our sadness at the consequences of the pandemic for humanity. (The Universal House of Justice, message dated 9 May 2020, to all National Spiritual Assemblies)

. . . assisting in endeavors to conserve the environment in ways which blend with the rhythm of life of our community must assume more importance in Bahá'í activities. (The Universal House of Justice, message dated 21 April 1989, to the Bahá'ís of the World, "Conservation of the Earth's Resources," *The Compilation of Compilations*, vol. I, p. 86)

A community school, for example, can in principle become a centre for activities such as agricultural production, health education, and family counselling. But, in most cases, it is advisable for it to start simply as a school, focusing all of its resources on the children it proposes to serve. (The Universal House of Justice, *Social Action*, 26 November 2012, to all National Spiritual Assemblies)

While eschewing partisan political activity, Bahá'ís are to vigorously engage in constructive public discourse and in a wide range of social endeavours aimed at the betterment of the world and the progress of their respective nations. They undertake such activities with humility, discernment and respect for prevailing laws and social conditions, in a spirit of learning and in collaboration with like-minded groups and individuals, fully confident in the power inherent in the principle of unity in diversity and in the efficacy of mutual aid and cooperation. (From a letter written on behalf of the Universal House of Justice, dated 22 January 2010, to an individual)

When the Bahá'í community in a village is a significant proportion of the population, it has a wide range of opportunities to be an example and an encouragement of means of improving the quality of life in the village (From a letter written on behalf of the Universal House of Justice, dated 25 July 1988, to a National Spiritual Assembly, in Universal House of Justice, Research Department, *Agriculture and Rural Life*, 1995)

The vast majority of Bahá'í projects will be primarily generated at the grass roots, and, initially as required, will receive help from Bahá'í sources, in terms of finances and manpower. The projects will, as you have surmised, be non-profit making, concerned mainly with activities closely related to education, health and hygiene, agriculture and simple community development activities. (From a letter written on behalf of the Universal House of Justice, dated 22 December 1983, to an individual believer, in *Lights of Guidance*, no. 1879)

While as a fundamental principle Bahá'ís do not engage in partisan political affairs, this should not be interpreted in a manner that prevents the friends from full and active participation in the search for solutions to the pressing problems facing humanity. Given that the question of climate change gives rise to social, economic, and environmental concerns across the world, interested Bahá'ís and Bahá'í institutions and agencies have naturally addressed it, whether at local, regional, national, or international levels. However, this does not mean that conclusions about scientific findings on climate change associated with such initiatives should be construed or presented as matters of religious conviction or obligation. (From a letter written on behalf of the Universal House of Justice, dated 29 November 2017, to three individuals)

Your letter reflects thoughtful concern about the practical limits of scientific knowledge, its implications for public policy, and its possible misrepresentation in an argument warning about catastrophic anthropogenic climate change that you feel is extreme, political, and unjustified by the facts. Although you do not mention it, you are surely aware that your measured skepticism is largely overshadowed in the public debate by another extreme perspective, promoted by political and vested interests, that goes as far as denying climate change and attempting to dismiss or contend with relevant scientific findings. Specific concerns about possible extremes on one side of the debate, therefore, must be addressed without appearing to advocate the other extreme. On the matter of climate change and other vital issues with profound implications for the common good,

Bahá'ís have to avoid being drawn into the all too common tendencies evident in contemporary discourse to delineate sharp dichotomies, become ensnared in contests for power, and engage in intractable debate that obstructs the search for viable solutions to the world's problems. Humanity would be best and most effectively served by setting aside partisan disputation, pursuing united action that is informed by the best available scientific evidence and grounded in spiritual principles, and thoughtfully revising action in the light of experience. The incessant focus on generating and magnifying points of difference rather than building upon points of agreement leads to exaggeration that fuels anger and confusion, thereby diminishing the will and capacity to act on matters of vital concern. (From a letter written on behalf of the Universal House of Justice, dated 29 November 2017, to three individuals)

A moderate perspective is a practical and principled standpoint from which one can recognize and adopt valid and insightful ideas whatever their source, without prejudice. "Whoso cleaveth to justice, can, under no circumstances, transgress the limits of moderation," Bahá'u'lláh states. "He discerneth the truth in all things, through the guidance of Him Who is the All-Seeing." (From a letter written on behalf of the Universal House of Justice, dated 29 November 2017, to three individuals)

By moderation, Bahá'u'lláh is in no way referring to mere compromise, the dilution of truth, or a hypocritical or utopian consensus. The moderation He calls for demands an end to destructive excesses that have plagued humanity and fomented ceaseless contention and turmoil. (From a letter written on behalf of the Universal House of Justice, dated 29 November 2017, to three individuals)

. . . there are "a great many Bahá'ís who are engaged as individuals in social action and public discourse through their occupations." Every believer has the opportunity to examine the forces operating in society and introduce relevant aspects of the teachings within the discourses prevalent in whatever social space he or she is present. (From a letter written on behalf of the Universal House of Justice, dated 24 July 2013, to the National Spiritual Assembly of Canada)

Whenever Bahá'ís do participate in activities associated with this topic [climate change] in the wider society, they can help to contribute to a constructive process by elevating the discourse above partisan concerns and self-interest to strive to achieve unity of thought and action. A range of Bahá'í concepts can inform these efforts; the letter of the House of Justice dated 1 March 2017, for example, addresses moral questions of consumption and excessive materialism that are associated with the exploitation and degradation of the environment. (From a letter written on behalf of the Universal House of Justice, dated 29 November 2017, to three individuals)

It will be apparent that the precepts the friends observe in the course of their general interactions with those around them must also characterize, sometimes even more scrupulously, their communication carried out via social media. These precepts include the prohibition on backbiting, the counsel to see the world with their own eyes and not through the eyes of others, the need to uphold the oneness of humanity and avoid a mind-set of "us" and "them," and the principles of consultation and the necessary decorum associated with it.

The friends will occasionally come across instances when their fellow believers have made comments or circulated the comments of others in ways that seem unwise, or imprudent, when judged against the standards set out in the Bahá'í Writings. It would be wrong, when encountering postings of this kind, to conclude that such behaviour must therefore be unobjectionable, condoned, or even encouraged. Not infrequently, Bahá'í institutions have had to counsel individuals about their actions online, although wherever possible they do so with discretion, out of respect for the dignity of the persons in question. (From a letter written on behalf of the Universal House of Justice, dated 1 December 2019, to all National Spiritual Assemblies)

Openness to collaboration with people of capacity and leaders of thought concerned with issues of progress, and willingness and ability to invite them to participate in applying the Teachings to specific problems, have to be created at all levels, if we are to fully exploit this dimension of our development endeavors. *(Bahá'í Social And Economic Development: Prospects for the Future,* 16 September 1993. A statement approved by the Universal House of Justice for use in orienting and guiding the work of Bahá'í social and economic development throughout the world)

Social and economic development requires the flow of resources, both material and intellectual. Bahá'í communities are linked by institutions and agencies at the local, regional, national, continental, and international levels, each committed to upholding the principle of the oneness of humankind. These institutional arrangements allow for resources to flow in a structured and systematic manner, and communities in rural areas as well as in highly industrialized regions benefit equally from them. The practice of dividing the world into dichotomous groups of "the developed" and "the underdeveloped," of "the advanced" and "the backward," is foreign to Bahá'í efforts in the field of development—indeed, to all Bahá'í endeavours. (*Social*

Action. A paper prepared by the Office of Social and Economic Development at the Bahá'í World Center, 26 November 2012)

Interpersonal relations between the constituent elements of a village have a crucial effect on rural development. When unity and co-operation exists between families and households, agricultural machinery can be shared and used most effectively, a diversity of specialized skills can be fostered and used to mutual advantage, and the detrimental effects of adverse weather and farm animal disease are minimized. Such unity cannot be legislated, but must rest on a commitment to the welfare of the entire village together with a sincere and lasting affection for all the members of the village. (Bahá'í International Community, "Spiritual and Social Values for Rural Development," paper presented to the Twentieth Conference of the South Pacific Commission Port Moresby, Papua New Guinea, 18 October 1980)

While individuals must do their utmost to provide for themselves and their dependents, the community must accept responsibility, when necessary, to help meet basic needs. Access to development programs and their benefits must be ensured for all. (Bahá'í International Community, "Valuing Spirituality in Development: Initial Considerations Regarding the Creation of Spiritually Based Indicators for Development." A concept paper written for the World Faiths and Development Dialogue, Lambeth Palace, London, 18–19 February 1998)

Only discourse at the level of principle has the power to invoke a moral commitment, which will, in turn, make possible the discovery of enduring solutions to the many challenges confronting a rapidly integrating human society . . . the Earth Charter can tap a powerful source of individual and collective motivation, which will be essential for the reorientation of the world toward a sustainable future. (Bahá'í International Community, "The Earth Charter/Rio De Janeiro Declaration and the Oneness of Humanity," UN, 1997)

The Bahá'í International Community, convenor of the "Advocates for African Food Security: lessening the burden for women," welcomes the opportunity to once again address the 35th session of the Commission on the Status of Women. The "Advocates" was formed following a UNIFEM-initiated symposium on African women farmers held concurrently with the Special Session of the United Nations General Assembly in 1986 on the Critical Economic Situation in Africa. The Advocates' objective is to stimulate action to maintain a global focus on the critical role of women in all the activities that countries feel are necessary for achieving full food security. Membership in the Advocates has expanded from the fourteen founding organizations to over thirty. It is a unique group in that it includes NGOs (non-governmental organizations) working in cooperation with representatives of United Nations bodies, governments and intergovernmental organizations working together on an equal status basis. Activities focus on practical ways to lessen the burden of women in the areas of food, health, water, and energy in order to improve the quality of their lives generally and to free their potential to produce crops, not only for their families, but for national food security. . . . The Advocates take the opportunity once again to urge the Commission:

> to support African women's perspectives in dialogues among UN agencies, governments and NGOs in the search for improved methods of popular participation in African recovery and food security;

to ensure active participation of women in policy formulation and provide appropriate channels for information exchange in all aspects of food security, including land tenure, water, energy, environment and health; to encourage men to recognize and support the valuable contribution of African women farmers to food security and impress upon them that food security is the business of everyone in the community; to urge UN agencies, governments and NGOs to recognize and utilize grassroots knowledge and traditional methods when introducing appropriate and new technology; to urge governments to include the actual work done by African women farmers in statistical reporting for the GNP; to identify, advocate and urge the incorporation of environmentally sound policy strategies which promote sustainable development in Africa.

In this respect, we take note of preparations for the second World Conference on the Environment in 1992 and urge the Commission to insure that the concerns of women farmers are taken into account; to identify local African organizations working with and for women farmers and support their efforts; and to press elected representatives and policymakers to favor those programmes that directly lessen the burdens of the African woman farmer. (Bahá'í International Community, "Advocates for African Food Security: Lessening the Burden for Women, Joint statement to the 35th session of the United Nations Commission on the Status of Women," 27 February 1991)

Once the domain of scientists and negotiators, the discourse on climate change has become a core part of informed debates about the future direction of the affairs of humankind. . . . To contribute to this important discourse, we assert that the principle of the oneness of humankind must become the ruling principle of international life. This principle does not seek to undermine national autonomy or suppress cultural or intellectual diversity. Rather, it makes it possible to view the climate change challenge through a new lens—one that perceives humanity as a unified whole, not unlike the cells of the human body, infinitely differentiated in form and function yet united in a common purpose which exceeds that of its component parts. This principle constitutes more than a call for cooperation; it seeks to remold anachronistic and unjust patterns of human interaction in a manner that reflects the relationships that bind us as members of one human race. The earnest consideration of the place of this principle in international relations should not be seen as an abstract exercise; it is precisely this level of analysis that must be undertaken and this level of commitment secured in order to forge a coherent ethic for the resolution of the climate change crisis. In order to progress beyond a world community driven by a largely economic and utilitarian calculus, to one of shared responsibility for the prosperity of all nations, such a principle must take root in the conscience of the individual. In this way, we come to recognize the broader human agenda—which subsumes those of climate change, poverty eradication, gender equality, development, and the like—and seeks to use both human and natural resources in a way that facilitates the progress and well-being of all people. (Bahá'í International Community, "Seizing the Opportunity: Redefining the challenge of climate change, Initial Considerations of the Bahá'í International Community," 1 December 2008)

PART 2

KNOWLEDGE

When populations engage in scientific inquiry coupled with a vibrant religious life, disintegrative processes based in superstition and materialism give way to a new reality.

KNOWLEDGE

O Son of Spirit! The best beloved of all things in My sight is Justice; turn not away therefrom if thou desirest Me, and neglect it not that I may confide in thee. By its aid thou shalt see with thine own eyes and not through the eyes of others, and shalt know of thine own knowledge and not through the knowledge of thy neighbor. Ponder this in thy heart; how it behooveth thee to be. Verily justice is My gift to thee and the sign of My loving-kindness. Set it then before thine eyes. (Bahá'u'lláh, The Hidden Words, Arabic, no. 2)

Immerse yourselves in the ocean of My words, that ye may unravel its secrets, and discover all the pearls of wisdom that lie hid in its depths. (Bahá'u'lláh, *Gleanings from the Writings of Bahá'u'lláh*, no. 70.2)

O My servants! Be as resigned and submissive as the earth, that from the soil of your being there may blossom the fragrant, the holy and multicolored hyacinths of My knowledge. (Bahá'u'lláh, *Gleanings from the Writings of Bahá'u'lláh*, no. 152.1)

From that which hath been said it becometh evident that all things, in their inmost reality, testify to the revelation of the names and attributes of God within them. Each according to its capacity, indicateth, and is expressive of, the knowledge of God. So potent and universal is this revelation, that it hath encompassed all things visible and invisible. (Bahá'u'lláh, *Gleanings from the Writings of Bahá'u'lláh*, no. 150.2)

Everyone, whether man or woman, should hand over to a trusted person a portion of what he or she earneth through trade, agriculture or other occupation, for the training and education of children. (Bahá'u'lláh, *Tablets of Bahá'u'lláh*, p. 90)

The Great Being saith: The learned of the day must direct the people to acquire those branches of knowledge which are of use, that both the learned themselves and the generality of mankind may derive benefits therefrom. Such academic pursuits as begin and end in words alone have never been and will never be of any worth. (Bahá'u'lláh, *Tablets of Bahá'u'lláh*, p. 11)

Arts, crafts and sciences uplift the world of being, and are conducive to its exaltation. Knowledge is as wings to man's life, and a ladder for his ascent. Its acquisition is incumbent upon everyone. The knowledge of such sciences, however, should be acquired as can profit the peoples of the earth, and not those which begin with words and end with words. Great indeed is the claim of scientists and craftsmen on the peoples of the world. (Bahá'u'lláh, *Epistle to the Son of the Wolf*, p. 26)

How vast the number of people who are well versed in every science, yet it is their adherence to the holy Word of God which will determine their faith, inasmuch as the fruit of every science is none other than the knowledge of divine precepts and submission unto

His good-pleasure. (The Báb, *Selections from the Writings of the Báb*, no. 3.14.1)

For knowledge is light, life, felicity, perfection, and beauty, and causes the soul to draw nigh to the divine threshold. It is the honor and glory of the human realm and the greatest of God's bounties. Knowledge is identical to guidance, and ignorance is the essence of error. Happy are those who spend their days in the pursuit of knowledge, in the discovery of the secrets of the universe, and in the meticulous investigation of truth! ('Abdu'l-Bahá, *Some Answered Questions*, no. 34.9)

. . . education cannot alter the inner essence of a man, but it doth exert tremendous influence, and with this power it can bring forth from the individual whatever perfections and capacities are deposited within him. A grain of wheat, when cultivated by the farmer, will yield a whole harvest, and a seed, through the gardener's care, will grow into a great tree. ('Abdu'l-Bahá, *Selections from the Writings of 'Abdu'l-Bahá*, no. 104.2)

Exert every effort in the fields of development and of civilization, in the acquisition of knowledge, the increase of trade, the improvement of agriculture and the promotion of modern discoveries. ('Abdu'l-Bahá from a tablet translated from the Persian. Universal House of Justice, Research Department, *Agriculture and Rural Life*, 1995)

See how, in this day, the scope of sciences and arts hath widened out, and what wondrous technical advances have been made, and to what a high degree the mind's powers have increased, and what stupendous inventions have appeared. This age is indeed as a hundred other ages: should ye gather the yield of a hundred ages, and set that against the accumulated product of our times, the yield of this one era will prove greater than that of a hundred gone before. ('Abdu'l-Bahá, *Selections from the Writings of 'Abdu'l-Bahá*, no. 73.5)

... education is of three kinds: material, human, and spiritual. Material education aims at the growth and development of the body, and consists in securing its sustenance and obtaining the means of its ease and comfort. This education is common to both man and animal.

Human education, however, consists in civilization and progress, that is, sound governance, social order, human welfare, commerce and industry, arts and sciences, momentous discoveries, and great undertakings. . . .

As to divine education, it is the education of the Kingdom and consists in acquiring divine perfections. ('Abdu'l-Bahá, *Some Answered Questions*, no. 3.5–7)

Little reflection, little admonition is necessary for us to realize the purpose of our creation. What a heavenly potentiality God has deposited within us! What a power God has given our spirits! He has endowed us with a power to penetrate the realities of things; but we must be self-abnegating, we must have pure spirits, pure intentions, and strive with heart and soul while in the human world to attain everlasting glory. ('Abdu'l-Bahá, *The Promulgation of Universal Peace*, p. 261)

The gentleman then put a question which he said he considered of very great importance in connection with a religious movement, claiming to be universal. What position he asked, if any, did Bahá'u'lláh given to the modern ideas and conceptions of Science in his teachings. The whole structure of modern civilization is based upon the results and the knowledge obtained through laborious and patient observation of facts collected by men of Science: in some cases through hundreds of years of painstaking investigation. . . . 'Abdu'l-Bahá replied that a very great importance was given to Science and knowledge in the writings of Bahá'u'lláh, who wrote that, if a man educated the children of the poor, who could not themselves afford to do so, it was, in the sight of God, as if he had educated the Son of God. If any religion rejected Science and knowledge, that religion was false. Science and Religion should go forward together; indeed, they should be like two fingers of one hand. ('Abdu'l-Bahá, *'Abdu'l-Bahá in London*, p. 71)

Religion and science are the two wings upon which man's intelligence can soar into the heights, with which the human soul can progress. It is not possible to fly with one wing alone! Should a man try to fly with the wing of religion alone he would quickly fall into the quagmire of superstition, whilst on the other hand, with the wing of science alone he would also make no progress, but fall into the despairing slough of materialism. ('Abdu'l-Bahá, *Paris Talks*, no. 44.14)

God made religion and science to be the measure, as it were, of our understanding. Take heed that you neglect not such a wonderful power. Weigh all things in this balance. . . . Put all your beliefs into harmony with science; there can be no opposition, for truth is one. ('Abdu'l-Bahá, *Paris Talks*, no. 44.21)

Study the sciences, acquire more and more knowledge. Assuredly one may learn to the end of one's life! Use your knowledge always for the benefit of others; so may war cease on the face of this beautiful earth, and a glorious edifice of peace and concord be raised. Strive that your high ideals may be realized in the Kingdom of God on earth, as they will be in Heaven. ('Abdu'l-Bahá, *Paris Talks*, no. 11.13)

Shoghi Effendi has for years urged the Bahá'ís (who asked his advice, and in general also) to study history, economics, sociology, etc., in order to be au courant with all the progressive movements and thoughts being put forth today, and so that they could correlate these to the Bahá'í teachings. What he wants the Bahá'ís to do is to study more, not to study less. The more general knowledge, scientific and otherwise, they possess, the better. Likewise he is constantly urging them to really study the Bahá'í teachings more deeply. One might liken Bahá'u'lláh's teachings to a sphere; there are points poles apart, and in between the thoughts and doctrines that unite them. (From a letter written on behalf of Shoghi Effendi, dated 5 July 1947, to an individual believer, in *Science and Technology*, compiled by Research Department of the Universal House of Justice.)

. . . science and religion are two complementary systems of knowledge and practice by which human beings come to understand the world around them and through which civilization advances; that religion without science soon degenerates into superstition and fanaticism, while science without religion becomes the tool of crude materialism. . . . (The Universal House of Justice, message dated 2 March 2013, to the Bahá'ís of Iran)

The believers must guard against seizing upon any particular text which may appeal to them and which they may only partially or even incorrectly understand. . . . (From a letter written on behalf of the Universal House of Justice, dated 24 January 1977, to an individual believer)

Scientific inquiry into the question of human contributions to global warming has gradually unfolded over a century of investigation and, more recently, with intense scrutiny. While there will naturally be differences of view among individual scientists, there does exist at present a striking degree of agreement among experts in relevant fields about the cause and impact of climate change. Sound scientific results, obtained through the employment of sound scientific methods, produce knowledge that can be acted upon; ultimately, the outcomes of action must stand the test of further scientific inquiry and the objective facts of the physical world. . . . (From a letter written on behalf of the Universal House of Justice, dated 29 November 2017, to three individuals)

That the development process is inherently complex is undeniable. It can involve activity in areas such as agriculture and animal husbandry, manufacturing and marketing, the management of funds and natural resources, health and sanitation, education and socialization, communication and community organization. The knowledge that must be brought to bear on the development concerns of the communities of the world, then, does not fit into a single area or discipline. Interdisciplinary and multisectoral action is clearly called for. Yet the capacity to pursue such coordinated action will only appear in the Bahá'í community over the course of decades, as will the capacity to address development issues at increasingly higher levels of complexity and effectiveness. (*Social Action*. A paper prepared by the Office of Social and Economic Development at the Bahá'í World Center, 26 November 2012)

Social action, of whatever size and complexity, should strive to remain free of simplistic and distorted conceptions of science and religion. To this end, an imaginary duality between reason and faith—a duality that would confine reason to the realm of empirical evidence and logical argumentation and which would associate faith with superstition and irrational thought—must be avoided. The process of development has to be rational and systematic—incorporating, for example, scientific capabilities of observing, of measuring, of rigorously testing ideas—and at the same time deeply aware of faith and spiritual convictions. In the words of 'Abdu'l-Bahá: "faith compriseth both knowledge and the performance of good works." (*Social Action*. A paper prepared by the Office of Social and Economic Development at the Bahá'í World Center, 26 November 2012)

Reality is one, and when truth is investigated and ascertained, it will lead to individual and collective progress. In the quest for truth, science and religion—the two systems of knowledge available to humankind—must closely and continuously interact. The insights and skills that represent scientific accomplishment must look to the force of spiritual commitment and moral principle to ensure their appropriate application. (Bahá'í International Community, "Valuing Spirituality in Development: Initial Considerations Regarding the Creation of Spiritually Based Indicators for Development." A concept paper written for the World Faiths and Development Dialogue, Lambeth Palace, London, 18–19 February 1998)

This question of institutional capacity (e.g. the establishment of regional centers of research and training) constitutes a major challenge to sustainable development. If successfully met, however, the result will be to break the present unbalanced flow of knowledge in the world and dissociate development from ill-conceived processes of modernization. "Modern" technologies will be characterized by an orientation towards addressing locally defined needs and by priorities that take into account both the material and moral prosperity of society as a whole. (Bahá'í International Community, "Rethinking Prosperity: Forging Alternatives to a Culture of Consumerism," 2010)

For example, despite the fact that most agricultural work in developing countries is carried out by low-income women, the primary shapers and users of agricultural technologies have been men. A key challenge is how to strengthen women's capacities to identify technological needs, and to create and adapt technologies in light of social needs and resource constraints. Reforming the present flow of knowledge—from 'North' to 'South'; from urban to rural; from men to women—will free development from narrowly conceived conceptions of modernization. (Bahá'í International Community, "Contribution to the 56th Session of the United Nations Commission on the Status of Women," New York, 27 February 2012)

RELIGION

Gather ye together with the utmost joy and fellowship and recite the verses revealed by the merciful Lord. By so doing the doors to true knowledge will be opened to your inner beings, and ye will then feel your souls endowed with steadfastness and your hearts filled with radiant joy. (Bahá'u'lláh, from a Tablet—translated from the Arabic, in *Prayer and Devotional Life*, no. 68)

O people! Consort with the followers of all religions in a spirit of friendliness and fellowship. (Bahá'u'lláh, *Tablets of Bahá'u'lláh*, p. 87)

The Bahá'í Faith recognizes the unity of God and of His Prophets, upholds the principle of an unfettered search after truth, condemns all forms of superstition and prejudice, teaches that the fundamen-

97

tal purpose of religion is to promote concord and harmony, that it must go hand-in-hand with science, and that it constitutes the sole and ultimate basis of a peaceful, an ordered and progressive society. (Shoghi Effendi, letter dated June 1933, to the High Commissioner for Palestine, in *Science and Technology*, compiled by the Research Department of the Universal House of Justice)

To them will the Ma_sh_riqu'l-A_dh_kár symbolize the fundamental verity underlying the Bahá'í Faith, that religious truth is not absolute but relative, that Divine Revelation is not final but progressive. (Shoghi Effendi, *Bahá'í Administration*, p. 185)

A Bahá'í who has studied the Teachings of Bahá'u'lláh, who has accepted His claim to be the Manifestation of God for this Age, and who has seen His Teachings at work in his daily life, knows as the result of rational investigation, confirmed by actual experience, that true religion, far from being the product solely of human striving after truth, is the fruit of the creative Word of God which, with divine power, transforms human thought and action. (The Universal House of Justice, message dated 3 January 1979, to the Participants in the Bahá'í Studies Seminar held in Cambridge on 30 September and 1 October 1978)

Writing of religion as a social force, Bahá'u'lláh said: Religion is the greatest of all means for the establishment of order in the world and for the peaceful contentment of all that dwell therein Referring to the eclipse or corruption of religion, he wrote: "Should the lamp of religion be obscured, chaos and confusion will ensue, and the lights of fairness, of justice, of tranquility and peace cease to shine." (The Universal House of Justice, *The Promise of World Peace*, 1985, To the Peoples of the World)

"There can be no doubt whatever," Bahá'u'lláh asserts, "that the peoples of the world, of whatever race or religion, derive their inspiration from one heavenly Source, and are the subjects of one God." He explains that the Founders of the world religions, the great universal Educators of humanity, share a common purpose to unite humanity and ensure the advancement of civilization. "They all abide in the same tabernacle, soar in the same heaven, are seated upon the same throne, utter the same speech, and proclaim the same Faith." He urges the peoples of the world to "consort with the followers of all religions in a spirit of friendliness and fellowship." And He further states: That the divers communions of the earth, and the manifold systems of religious belief, should never be allowed to foster the feelings of animosity among men, is, in this Day, of the essence of the Faith of God and His Religion. These principles and laws, these firmly established and mighty systems, have proceeded from one Source, and are the rays of one Light. That they differ one from another is to be attributed to the varying requirements of the ages in which they were promulgated. . . .

'Abdu'l-Bahá stresses that "the divine religions must be the cause of oneness among men, and the means of unity and love; they must promulgate universal peace, free man from every prejudice, bestow joy and gladness, exercise kindness to all men and do away with every difference and distinction." He furthermore observes that "religion must be the cause of fellowship and love. If it becomes the cause of estrangement then it is not needed, for religion is like a remedy; if it aggravates the disease then it becomes unnecessary." (From a letter written on behalf of the Universal House of Justice, dated 27 December 2017, to an individual)

The purpose of true religion, then, is to produce good fruits, and if, in the name of religion, conflict, prejudice, and hatred are engendered among humanity, this is due to fallible human interpretations and impositions that can be overcome by seeking the divine truth that lies at the heart of every religion. "May fanaticism and religious bigotry be unknown," He urges, "all humanity enter the bond of brotherhood, souls consort in perfect agreement, the nations of earth at last hoist the banner of truth, and the religions of the world enter the divine temple of oneness, for the foundations of the heavenly religions are one reality." (From a letter written on behalf of the Universal House of Justice, dated 27 December 2017, to an individual)

Of particular note is the role to be played by religious faith. Religion has been a feature of human civilization since the dawn of recorded history, and has prompted countless multitudes to arise and exert themselves for the well-being of others. Religion offers an understanding of human existence and development that lifts the eye from the rocky path to the distant horizon. And when true to the spirit of its transcendent founders, religion has been one of the most powerful forces for the creation of new and beneficial patterns of individual and collective life. (Bahá'í International Community, "Shared Vision, Shared Volition: Choosing Our Global Future Together," a statement of the Bahá'í International Community to the United Nations Climate Change Conference in Paris, France, 23 November 2015)

There is perhaps no more powerful impetus for social change than religion. Bahá'u'lláh said: "Religion is the greatest of all means for the establishment of order in the world and for the peaceful contentment of all that dwell therein." In attempting to build a new ecological ethic, the teachings of all religious traditions can play a role in helping to inspire their followers. (Bahá'í International Community, "The Bahá'í Statement on Nature," 1987)

Bahá'í Scriptures teach that, as trustees of the planet's vast resources and biological diversity, humanity must seek to protect the "heritage [of] future generations;" see in nature a reflection of the divine; approach the earth, the source of material bounties, with humility; temper its actions with moderation; and be guided by the fundamental spiritual truth of our age, the oneness of humanity. The speed and facility with which we establish a sustainable pattern of life will depend, in the final analysis, on the extent to which we are willing to be transformed, through the love of God and obedience to His Laws, into constructive forces in the process of creating an ever-advancing civilization. (Bahá'í International Community, "Conservation and Sustainable Development in the Bahá'í Faith," paper presented by the Bahá'í International Community to the Summit on the Alliance Between Religions and Conservation, 3 May 1995)

Given their tremendous capacity to mobilize public opinion and their extensive reach in the most remote communities around the world, religious communities and their leaders bear an inescapable and weighty role in the climate change arena. By many measures, increasing numbers of religious communities are consistently lending their voice and resources to efforts to mitigate and adapt to the effects of climate change—they are educating their constituencies, providing a scriptural basis for ethical action and leading or participating in efforts at the national and international levels. (Bahá'í International Community, "Seizing the Opportunity: Redefining the challenge of climate change, Initial Considerations of the Bahá'í International Community," 1 December 2008)

CREATOR

To every discerning and illuminated heart it is evident that God, the unknowable Essence, the Divine Being, is immensely exalted beyond every human attribute, such as corporeal existence, ascent and descent, egress and regress. (Bahá'u'lláh, *Gleanings from the Writings of Bahá'u'lláh*, no. 19.1)

Say: In this day, the fertilizing winds of the grace of God have passed over all things. Every creature hath been endowed with all the potentialities it can carry. And yet the peoples of the world have denied this grace! Every tree hath been endowed with the choicest fruits, every ocean enriched with the most luminous gems. Man, himself, hath been invested with the gifts of understanding and knowledge. The whole creation hath been made the recipient of the revelation of the All-Merciful, and the earth the repository of things inscrutable to all except God, the Truth, the Knower of things unseen. The time is approaching when every created thing will have cast its burden. Glorified be God Who hath vouchsafed this grace that encompasseth all things, whether seen or unseen! Thus have We created the whole earth anew in this day, yet most of the people have failed to perceive it. Say: The grace of God can never be adequately understood; how much less can His own Self, the Help in Peril, the Self-Subsisting, be comprehended! (Bahá'u'lláh, "Súriy-i-Haykal," *The Summons of the Lord of Hosts*, no. 1.47)

It is in Our power, should We wish it, to enable a speck of floating dust to generate, in less than the twinkling of an eye, suns of infinite, of unimaginable splendor, to cause a dewdrop to develop into vast and numberless oceans, to infuse into every letter such a force as to empower it to unfold all the knowledge of past and future ages. This, in truth, is a matter simple of accomplishment. Such have been the evidences of My power from the beginning that hath no beginning until the end that hath no end. (Bahá'u'lláh, "Súriy-i-Haykal," *The Summons of the Lord of Hosts*, no. 1.75)

It is clear and evident, therefore, that the first bestowal of God is the Word, and its discoverer and recipient is the power of understanding. This Word is the foremost instructor in the school of existence and the revealer of Him Who is the Almighty. All that is seen is visible only through the light of its wisdom. All that is manifest is but a token of its knowledge. All names are but its name, and the beginning and end of all matters must needs depend upon it. (Bahá'u'lláh, "Lawḥ-i-Mánikchí-Ṣáḥib," *Tabernacle of Unity*, no. 1.2)

Whatever is in the heavens and whatever is on the earth is a direct evidence of the revelation within it of the attributes and names of God, inasmuch as within every atom are enshrined the signs that bear eloquent testimony to the revelation of that Most Great Light. (Bahá'u'lláh, *Gleanings from the Writings of Bahá'u'lláh*, no. 40.1)

A drop of the billowing ocean of His endless mercy hath adorned all creation with the ornament of existence, and a breath wafted from His peerless Paradise hath invested all beings with the robe of His sanctity and glory. A sprinkling from the unfathomed deep of His sovereign and all-pervasive Will hath, out of utter nothingness, called into being a creation which is infinite in its range and deathless in its duration. The wonders of His bounty can never cease, and the stream of His merciful grace can never be arrested. The process of His creation hath had no beginning, and can have no end. (Bahá'u'lláh, *Gleanings from the Writings of Bahá'u'lláh*, no. 26.2)

Know thou that every created thing is a sign of the revelation of God. Each, according to its capacity, is, and will ever remain, a token of the Almighty. Inasmuch as He, the sovereign Lord of all, hath willed to reveal His sovereignty in the kingdom of names and attributes, each and every created thing hath, through the act of the Divine Will, been made a sign of His glory. So pervasive and general is this revelation that nothing whatsoever in the whole universe can be discovered that doth not reflect His splendor. Under such conditions every consideration of proximity and remoteness is obliterated. . . . Were the Hand of Divine power to divest of this high endowment all created things, the entire universe would become desolate and void. (Bahá'u'lláh, *Gleanings from the Writings of Bahá'u'lláh*, no. 93.1)

Love is the most great law that ruleth this mighty and heavenly cycle, the unique power that bindeth together the divers elements of this material world, the supreme magnetic force that directeth the movements of the spheres in the celestial realms. ('Abdu'l-Bahá, *Selections from the Writings of 'Abdu'l-Bahá*, no. 12.1)

Likewise, look into this endless universe: a universal power inevitably existeth, which encompasseth all, directing and regulating all the parts of this infinite creation; and were it not for this Director, this Coordinator, the universe would be flawed and deficient. It would be even as a madman; whereas ye can see that this endless creation carrieth out its functions in perfect order, every separate part of it performing its own task with complete reliability, nor is there any flaw to be found in all its workings. Thus it is clear that a Universal Power existeth, directing and regulating this infinite universe. Every rational mind can grasp this fact. ('Abdu'l-Bahá, *Selections from the Writings of 'Abdu'l-Bahá*, no. 21.8)

We declare that love is the cause of the existence of all phenomena and that the absence of love is the cause of disintegration or nonexistence. Love is the conscious bestowal of God, the bond of affiliation in all phenomena. ('Abdu'l-Bahá, *The Promulgation of Universal Peace*, p. 356)

The Báb hath said: "Should a tiny ant desire, in this day, to be possessed of such power as to be able to unravel the abstrusest and most bewildering passages of the Qur'án, its wish will no doubt be fulfilled, inasmuch as the mystery of eternal might vibrates within the innermost being of all created things." If so helpless a creature can be endowed with so subtle a capacity, how much more efficacious must be the power released through the liberal effusions of the grace of Bahá'u'lláh! (Shoghi Effendi, *The Advent of Divine Justice*, p. 46)

KINGDOMS OF CREATION

Nature in its essence is the embodiment of My Name, the Maker, the Creator. Its manifestations are diversified by varying causes, and in this diversity there are signs for men of discernment. Nature is God's Will and is its expression in and through the contingent world. It is a dispensation of Providence ordained by the Ordainer, the All-Wise. (Bahá'u'lláh, *Tablets of Bahá'u'lláh*, p. 9)

Look at the world and ponder a while upon it. It unveileth the book of its own self before thine eyes and revealeth that which the Pen of thy Lord, the Fashioner, the All-Informed, hath inscribed therein. It will acquaint thee with that which is within it and upon it and will give thee such clear explanations as to make thee independent of every eloquent expounder. (Bahá'u'lláh, *Tablets of Bahá'u'lláh*, p. 9)

Know thou that every created thing is a sign of the revelation of God. Each, according to its capacity, is, and will ever remain, a token of the Almighty. Inasmuch as He, the sovereign Lord of all, hath willed to reveal His sovereignty in the kingdom of names and attributes, each and every created thing hath, through the act of the Divine Will, been made a sign of His glory. So pervasive and general is this revelation that nothing whatsoever in the whole universe can be discovered that doth not reflect His splendor. Under such conditions every consideration of proximity and remoteness is obliterated. . . . Were the Hand of Divine power to divest of this high endowment all created things, the entire universe would become desolate and void. (Bahá'u'lláh, *Gleanings from the Writings of Bahá'u'lláh*, no. 93.1)

Know, verily, that the soul is a sign of God, a heavenly gem whose reality the most learned of men hath failed to grasp, and whose mystery no mind, however acute, can ever hope to unravel. It is the first among all created things to declare the excellence of its Creator, the first to recognize His glory, to cleave to His truth, and to bow down in adoration before Him. (Bahá'u'lláh, *Gleanings from the Writings of Bahá'u'lláh*, no. 82.1)

Know thou of a certainty that Love is the secret of God's holy Dispensation, the manifestation of the All-Merciful, the fountain of spiritual outpourings. Love is heaven's kindly light, the Holy Spirit's eternal breath that vivifieth the human soul. Love is the cause of God's revelation unto man, the vital bond inherent, in accordance with the divine creation, in the realities of things. ('Abdu'l-Bahá, *Selections from the Writings of 'Abdu'l-Bahá*, no. 12.1)

The existence of the Divine Being hath been clearly established, on the basis of logical proofs, but the reality of the Godhead is beyond the grasp of the mind. When thou dost carefully consider this matter, thou wilt see that a lower plane can never comprehend a higher. The mineral kingdom, for example, which is lower, is precluded from comprehending the vegetable kingdom; for the mineral, any such understanding would be utterly impossible. In the same way, no matter how far the vegetable kingdom may develop, it will achieve no conception of the animal kingdom, and any such comprehension at its level would be unthinkable, for the animal occupieth a plane higher than that of the vegetable: this tree cannot conceive of hearing and sight. And the animal kingdom, no matter how far it may evolve, can never become aware of the reality of the intellect, which discovereth the inner essence of all things, and comprehendeth those realities which cannot be seen; for the human plane as compared with that of the animal is very high. And although these beings all coexist in the contingent world, in each case the difference in their stations precludeth their grasp of the whole; for no lower degree can understand a higher, such comprehension being impossible.

The higher plane, however, understandeth the lower. The animal, for instance, comprehendeth the mineral and vegetable, the human understandeth the planes of the animal, vegetable and mineral. But the mineral cannot possibly understand the realms of man. And notwithstanding the fact that all these entities coexist in the phenomenal world, even so, no lower degree can ever comprehend a higher. ('Abdu'l-Bahá, *Selections from the Writings of 'Abdu'l-Bahá*, no. 21.2–3)

Nature is that condition or reality which outwardly is the source of the life and death, or, in other words, of the composition and decomposition, of all things. This nature is subject to a sound organization, to inviolable laws, to a perfect order, and to a consummate design, from which it never departs. To such an extent is this true that were you to gaze with the eye of insight and discernment, you would observe that all things—from the smallest invisible atom to the largest globes in the world of existence, such as the sun or the other great stars and luminous bodies—are most perfectly organized, be it with regard to their order, their composition, their outward form, or their motion, and that all are subject to one universal law from which

107

they never depart. When you consider nature itself, however, you see that it has neither awareness nor will. For instance, the nature of fire is to burn; it burns without consciousness or will. The nature of water is to flow; it flows without consciousness or will. The nature of the sun is to shed light; it shines without consciousness or will. The nature of vapour is to rise; it rises without consciousness or will. It is therefore evident that the natural movements of all created things are compelled, and that nothing moves of its own will save animals and, in particular, man. Man is able to resist and oppose nature inasmuch as he discovers the natures of things and, by virtue of this discovery, has mastery over nature itself. Indeed, all the crafts that man has devised proceed from this discovery. For example, he has invented the telegraph, which connects the East and the West. It is therefore evident that man rules over nature. ('Abdu'l-Bahá, *Some Answered Questions*, no. 1.2)

When we carefully investigate the kingdoms of existence and observe the phenomena of the universe about us, we discover the absolute order and perfection of creation. The dull minerals in their affinities, plants and vegetables with power of growth, animals in their instinct, man with conscious intellect and the heavenly orbs moving obediently through limitless space are all found subject to universal law, most complete, most perfect. ('Abdu'l-Bahá, *The Promulgation of Universal Peace*, p. 109)

If we look with a perceiving eye upon the world of creation, we find that all existing things may be classified as follows: first mineral—that is to say, matter or substance appearing in various forms of composition; second, vegetable—possessing the virtues of the mineral plus the power of augmentation or growth, indicating a degree higher and more specialized than the mineral; third, animal—pos-

108

sessing the attributes of the mineral and vegetable plus the power of sense perception; fourth, human—the highest specialized organism of visible creation, embodying the qualities of the mineral, vegetable and animal plus an ideal endowment absolutely absent in the lower kingdoms—the power of intellectual investigation into the mysteries of outer phenomena. ('Abdu'l-Bahá, *The Promulgation of Universal Peace*, pp. 39–40)

Know that nothing that exists remains in a state of repose—that is, all things are in motion. They are either growing or declining, either coming from non-existence into existence or passing from existence into non-existence. So this flower, this hyacinth, was for a time coming from non-existence into existence and is now passing from existence into non-existence. This is called essential or natural motion, and it can in no wise be dissociated from created things, for it is one of their essential requirements, just as it is an essential requirement of fire to burn. It is therefore clearly established that motion, whether advancing or declining, is necessary to existence. Now, as the human spirit continues after death, it must either advance or decline, and in the next world to cease to advance is the same as to decline. But the human spirit never transcends its own degree: It progresses only within that degree. For example, no matter how far the spirit and reality of Peter may progress, it will never reach the degree of the reality of Christ but will progress only within its own inherent limits. Thus, you see that however much this mineral may progress, its progress remains within its own degree; you cannot possibly bring this crystal, for example, to a state where it gains the power of sight. The moon, howsoever it may progress, can never become the shining sun, and its apogee and perigee will always remain within its own degree. And however far the Apostles might have progressed, they could never have become Christ. It is true that coal can become a diamond, but both are in the mineral degree and their constituent parts are the same. ('Abdu'l-Bahá, *Some Answered Questions*, no. 63.1)

. . . in the mineral kingdom the soil absorbs the air and the water and decomposes the creatures within it, and thus enables the existence of plants. The more microscopic animals exist in the soil, the better the plants will grow. And when the plant has grown, it is consumed by the animal, is incorporated in its body, and is endowed with a new existence. Thus it progresses further and assumes a higher reality than that which it initially possessed. This indeed is the means of progress and renewal from the mineral to the vegetable, from the vegetable to the animal, and from the animal to the human world. For as plants grow they are eaten by the animal and replace those elements which have been depleted in the latter's body. In this manner the plants enter the animal kingdom. The microscopic organisms in the air, water, and food enter in turn the body of man and replace that which has been assimilated therein.

Thus there is progress in these passages and renewals: The mineral passed from the mineral to the vegetable, then to the animal, and finally to the human realm. And were it not for the cycle of the eater and the eaten, no renewal would take place. Such a renewal, however, is one of the inherent requirements of existence, and all contingent things are bound to pass from one condition to another. ('Abdu'l-Bahá, *Pearls of Bounty*, no. 3.8.2–3)

Nature is the material world. When we look upon it, we see that it is dark and imperfect. For instance, if we allow a piece of land to remain in its natural condition, we will find it covered with thorns and thistles; useless weeds and wild vegetation will flourish upon it, and it will become like a jungle. The trees will be fruitless, lacking beauty and symmetry; wild animals, noxious insects and reptiles will abound in its dark recesses. This is the incompleteness and imperfection of the world of nature. To change these conditions, we must clear the ground and cultivate it so that flowers may grow instead of thorns and weeds—that is to say, we must illumine the dark world of nature. In their primal natural state, the forests are dim, gloomy, impenetrable. Man opens them to the light, clears away the tangled underbrush and plants fruitful trees. Soon the wild woodlands and jungle are changed into productive orchards and beautiful gardens; order has replaced chaos; the dark realm of nature has become illumined and brightened by cultivation. ('Abdu'l-Bahá, *The Promulgation of Universal Peace*, pp. 429–30)

In the physical creation, evolution is from one degree of perfection to another. The mineral passes with its mineral perfections to the vegetable; the vegetable, with its perfections, passes to the animal world, and so on to that of humanity. This world is full of seeming contradictions; in each of these kingdoms (mineral, vegetable and animal) life exists in its degree; though when compared to the life in a man, the earth appears to be dead, yet she, too, lives and has a life of her own. ('Abdu'l-Bahá, *Paris Talks*, no. 20.14)

Mineral

We declare that love is the cause of the existence of all phenomena and that the absence of love is the cause of disintegration or nonexistence. Love is the conscious bestowal of God, the bond of affiliation in all phenomena. We will first consider the proof of this through sense perception. As we look upon the universe, we observe that all composite beings or existing phenomena are made up primarily of single elements bound together by a power of attraction. Through this power of attraction cohesion has become manifest between atoms of these composing elements. The resultant being is a phenomenon of the lower contingent type. The power of cohesion expressed in the mineral kingdom is in reality love or affinity manifested in a low degree according to the exigencies of the mineral world. ('Abdu'l-Bahá, *The Promulgation of Universal Peace*, p. 356)

If attraction did not exist between the elements and among the cellular particles, the composition of that phenomenon would never have been possible. For instance, the stone is an existent phenomenon, a composition of elements. A bond of attraction has brought them together, and through this cohesion of ingredients this petrous object has been formed. This stone is the lowest degree of phenomena, but nevertheless within it a power of attraction is manifest without which the stone could not exist. This power of attraction in the mineral world is love, the only expression of love the stone can manifest. ('Abdu'l-Bahá, *The Promulgation of Universal Peace*, p. 374)

No matter how far a mineral may progress, it can never acquire the power of growth in the mineral kingdom. No matter how far this flower may progress, it can never manifest the power of sensation while it is in the vegetable kingdom. So this silver mineral can never gain sight or hearing; at most it can progress in its own degree and become a perfect mineral, but it cannot acquire the power of growth or sensation and can never become living: It can only progress in its own degree. ('Abdu'l-Bahá, *The Promulgation of Universal Peace*, p. 240)

When in the Gospels, Christ speaks of "water," He means *that which causes life*, for without water no worldly creature can live—mineral, vegetable, animal and man, one and all, depend upon water for their very being. Yes, the latest scientific discoveries prove to us that even mineral has some form of life, and that it also needs water for its existence. ('Abdu'l-Bahá, *Paris Talks*, no. 27.2)

The excellence, adornment, and perfection of the earth consist in this, that through the outpourings of the vernal showers it should become green and verdant; that plants should spring forth; that flowers and herbs should grow; that blossom-filled trees should produce an abundant yield and bring forth fresh and succulent fruit; that gardens should be arrayed; that meadows should be adorned; that plains and mountains should don an emerald robe; and that fields and bowers, villages and cities should be decked forth. This is the felicity of the mineral world. ('Abdu'l-Bahá, *Some Answered Questions*, no. 15.2)

Vegetable

The height of exaltation and perfection of the vegetable world consists in this, that a tree should stand tall beside a stream of fresh water, that a gentle breeze should blow and the sun bestow its warmth upon it, that a gardener should tend it, and that day by day it should grow and yield fruit. But its real felicity consists in progressing into the animal and human worlds and in replacing that which has been consumed in the bodies of animals and men. ('Abdu'l-Bahá, *Some Answered Questions*, no. 15.3)

. . . the forms and organisms of phenomenal being and existence in each of the kingdoms of the universe are myriad and numberless. The vegetable plane or kingdom, for instance, has its infinite variety of types and material structures of plant life each distinct and different within itself, no two exactly alike in composition and detail for there are no repetitions in nature, and the augmentative virtue cannot be confined to any given image or shape. Each leaf has its own particular identity so to speak, its own individuality as a leaf. . . . ('Abdu'l-Bahá, *The Promulgation of Universal Peace*, p. 397)

This diversity of type is apparent throughout the whole of nature. . . . Let us look . . . at the beauty in diversity, the beauty of harmony, and learn a lesson from the vegetable creation. If you behold a garden in which all the plants were the same as to form, color and perfume, it would not seem beautiful to you at all, but, rather, monotonous and dull. The garden which is pleasing to the eye and which makes the heart glad, is the garden in which are growing side by side flowers of every hue, form and perfume, and the joyous contrast of color is what makes for charm and beauty. So is it with trees. An orchard full of fruit trees is a delight; so is a plantation planted with many species of shrubs. It is just the diversity and variety that constitutes its charm; each flower, each tree, each fruit, beside being beautiful in itself, brings out by contrast the qualities of the others, and shows to advantage the special loveliness of each and all. ('Abdu'l-Bahá, *Paris Talks*, no. 15.3–5)

And when the plant has grown, it is consumed by the animal, is incorporated in its body, and is endowed with a new existence. Thus it progresses further and assumes a higher reality than that which it initially possessed. ('Abdu'l-Bahá, *Pearls of Bounty*, no. 3.8.2)

DESIRE TO EXPRESS TO HIS MAJESTY THE KING OR HIS MAJESTY'S REPRE-SENTATIVE AS WELL AS TO ASSEMBLED GUESTS MY HOPE WORK OF MEN OF TREES SO IMPORTANT FOR PROTECTION PHYSICAL WORLD AND HERITAGE FUTURE GENERATIONS MAY BE RICHLY BLESSED AND AT SAME TIME CON-STITUTE YET ANOTHER FORCE WORKING FOR PEACE AND BROTHERHOOD IN THIS SORELY TRIED DIVIDED WORLD. (Shoghi Effendi, cable dated 23 May 1951, to New Earth Luncheon, London, in Universal House of Justice, Research Department, *Economics, Agriculture, and Related Subjects,* p. 8)

DESIRE EXPRESS ADMIRATION YOUR ESSENTIALLY HUMANITARIAN WORK NOBLE OBJECTIVE RECLAIM DESERTS SPIRIT CO-OPERATION FOSTERED BY YOUR UNDERTAKINGS WISH YOU EVERY SUCCESS. (Shoghi Effendi, cable dated 21 May 1956, to World Forestry Charter Luncheon, London, in Universal House of Justice, Research Department, *Economics, Agriculture, and Related Subjects,* p. 8)

Animal

He should show kindness to animals, how much more unto his fellowman, to him who is endowed with the power of utterance. (Bahá'u'lláh, The Kitáb-i-Íqán, ¶214)

If ye should hunt with beasts or birds of prey, invoke ye the Name of God when ye send them to pursue their quarry; for then whatever they catch shall be lawful unto you, even should ye find it to have died. He, verily, is the Omniscient, the All-Informed. Take heed, however, that ye hunt not to excess. Tread ye the path of justice and equity in all things. Thus biddeth you He Who is the Dawning-place of Revelation, would that ye might comprehend. (Bahá'u'lláh, The Kitáb-i-Aqdas, ¶60)

I have read thy letter, wherein thou didst express astonishment at some of the laws of God, such as that concerning the hunting of innocent animal, creatures who are guilty of no wrong.

Be thou not surprised at this. Reflect upon the inner realities of the universe, the secret wisdoms involved, the enigmas, the inter-relationships, the rules that govern all. For every part of the universe is connected with every other part by ties that are very powerful and admit of no imbalance, nor any slackening whatever. In the physical realm of creation, all things are eaters and eaten: the plant drinketh in the mineral, the animal doth crop and swallow down the plant, man doth feed upon the animal, and the mineral devoureth the body of man ('Abdu'l-Bahá, *Selections from the Writings of 'Abdu'l-Bahá*, no. 137.1–2)

Whensoever thou dost examine, through a microscope, the water man drinketh, the air he doth breathe, thou wilt see that with every breath of air, man taketh in an abundance of animal life, and with every draught of water, he also swalloweth down a great variety of animals. How could it ever be possible to put a stop to this process? For all creatures are eaters and eaten, and the very fabric of life is reared upon this fact. Were it not so, the ties that interlace all created things within the universe would be unraveled. ('Abdu'l-Bahá, *Selections from the Writings of 'Abdu'l-Bahá*, no. 137.3)

Thus if a predatory animal devours another animal, the latter has in reality not been abased but has been decomposed and recomposed, found a renewed existence, and passed from one body to another. This motion and renewal of beings gives rise to the orderly arrangement and interconnectedness of all things, and were it not for these passages across the vegetable, animal, and human realms, the chain of being would be broken and the innate order of nature would be disrupted. ('Abdu'l-Bahá, *Pearls of Bounty*, no. 3.8.4)

Unless ye must, Bruise not the serpent in the dust, How much less wound a man. And if ye can, No ant should ye alarm, Much less a brother harm. ('Abdu'l-Bahá, *Selections from the Writings of 'Abdu'l-Bahá*, no. 206)

Briefly, it is not only their fellow human beings that the beloved of God must treat with mercy and compassion, rather must they show forth the utmost loving-kindness to every living creature. For in all physical respects, and where the animal spirit is concerned, the selfsame feelings are shared by animal and man. Man hath not grasped this truth, however, and he believeth that physical sensations are confined to human beings, wherefore is he unjust to the animals, and cruel.

And yet in truth, what difference is there when it cometh to physical sensations? The feelings are one and the same, whether ye inflict pain on man or on beast. There is no difference here whatever. And indeed ye do worse to harm an animal, for man hath a language, he can lodge a complaint, he can cry out and moan; if injured he can have recourse to the authorities and these will protect him from his aggressor. But the hapless beast is mute, able neither to express its hurt nor take its case to the authorities. If a man inflict a thousand ills upon a beast, it can neither ward him off with speech nor hale him into court. Therefore it is essential that ye show forth the utmost consideration to the animal, and that ye be even kinder to him than to your fellow-man.

Train your children from their earliest days to be infinitely tender and loving to animals. If an animal be sick, let the children try to heal it, if it be hungry, let them feed it, if thirsty, let them quench its thirst, if weary, let them see that it rests.

Most human beings are sinners, but the beasts are innocent. Surely those without sin should receive the most kindness and love—all except animals which are harmful, such as bloodthirsty wolves, such as poisonous snakes, and similar pernicious creatures, the reason being that kindness to these is an injustice to human beings and other animals as well. If for example, ye be tender-hearted toward a wolf, this is but tyranny to a sheep, for a wolf will destroy a whole flock of sheep. A rabid dog, if given the chance, can kill a thousand animals and men. Therefore, compassion shown to wild and ravening beasts is cruelty to the peaceful ones—and so the harmful must be dealt with. But to the blessed animals the utmost kindness must be shown, the more the better. Tenderness and loving kindness are basic principles of God's heavenly kingdom. Ye should most carefully bear this matter in mind. ('Abdu'l-Bahá, *Selections from the Writings of 'Abdu'l-Bahá*, no. 138.2–5)

The majority of the illnesses that afflict man also afflict animals, but the animal does not treat them through medicines. The animal's physician in the mountains and the wilderness is its powers of taste and smell. The sick animal smells the plants that grow in the wilderness, eats those that its smell and taste find to be sweet and fragrant, and is cured. The reason is this: When, for example, the sugar component in its body becomes deficient, it craves sweet things and thus eats of sweet-tasting plants, for nature so urges and guides it. Thus, as the animal eats things that are pleasing to its smell and taste, the sugar component increases and it regains its health. It is therefore evident that it is possible to cure illnesses by means of fruits and other foods. But as the science of medicine has not yet been perfected, this fact has not been fully understood. When this science reaches perfection, treatments will be administered with fragrant fruits and plants as well as with other foods, and with hot and cold waters of various temperatures. ('Abdu'l-Bahá, *Some Answered Questions*, no. 73.6)

Likewise, we observe that animals which have undergone training in their sphere of limitation will progress and advance unmistakably, become more beautiful in appearance and increase in intelligence. For instance, how intelligent and knowing the Arabian horse has become through training, even how polite this horse has become through education. ('Abdu'l-Bahá, *The Promulgation of Universal Peace*, p. 106)

Even over animals, music has an effect. For example: When they wish to take a camel over a desert road, they attach to him some bells, or they play upon a flute, and this sound prevents him from realizing the fatigue of the journey; his nerves are affected, but he does not have an increase of thought, he feels nothing but physical sensation. ('Abdu'l-Bahá, in *The Compilation of Compilations*, vol. II, no. 1422)

In the physical powers and senses, however, man and the animal are partners. In fact, the animal is often superior to man in sense perception. For instance, the vision of some animals is exceedingly keen and the hearing of others most acute. Consider the instinct of a dog how much greater than that of man. But, although the animal shares with man all the physical virtues and senses, a spiritual power has been bestowed upon man of which the animal is devoid. This is a proof that there is something in man above and beyond the endowment of the animal—a faculty and virtue peculiar to the human kingdom which is lacking in the lower kingdoms of existence. This is the spirit of man. ('Abdu'l-Bahá, *The Promulgation of Universal Peace*, p. 338)

Human

Having created the world and all that liveth and moveth therein, He, through the direct operation of His unconstrained and sovereign Will, chose to confer upon man the unique distinction and capacity to know Him and to love Him—a capacity that must needs be regarded as the generating impulse and the primary purpose underlying the whole of creation. . . . (Bahá'u'lláh, *Gleanings from the Writings of Bahá'u'lláh*, no. 27.2)

The soul of man is the sun by which his body is illumined, and from which it draweth its sustenance, and should be so regarded. (Bahá'u'lláh, *Gleanings from the Writings of Bahá'u'lláh*, no. 80.4)

How resplendent the luminaries of knowledge that shine in an atom, and how vast the oceans of wisdom that surge within a drop! To a supreme degree is this true of man, who, among all created things, hath been invested with the robe of such gifts, and hath been singled out for the glory of such distinction. For in him are potentially revealed all the attributes and names of God to a degree that no other created being hath excelled or surpassed. All these names and attributes are applicable to him. (Bahá'u'lláh, *Gleanings from the Writings of Bahá'u'lláh*, no. 90.1)

Know ye that the embodiment of liberty and its symbol is the animal. That which beseemeth man is submission unto such restraints as will protect him from his own ignorance, and guard him against the harm of the mischief-maker. Liberty causeth man to overstep the bounds of propriety, and to infringe on the dignity of his station. It debaseth him to the level of extreme depravity and wickedness. (Bahá'u'lláh, *Gleanings from the Writings of Bahá'u'lláh*, no. 159.2)

And among the teachings of Bahá'u'lláh is man's freedom, that through the ideal Power he should be free and emancipated from the captivity of the world of nature; for as long as man is captive to nature he is a ferocious animal, as the struggle for existence is one of the exigencies of the world of nature. This matter of the struggle for existence is the fountainhead of all calamities and is the supreme affliction. ('Abdu'l-Bahá, *Selections from the Writings of 'Abdu'l-Bahá*, no. 227.21)

Question: What do you say regarding the theory of the evolution of beings to which certain European philosophers subscribe?

Answer: We discussed this matter the other day, but we will speak of it again. Briefly, this question comes down to the originality or non-originality of the species, that is, whether the essence of the human species was fixed from the very origin or whether it subsequently came from the animals.

Certain European philosophers hold that species evolve and can even change and transform into other species. Among the proofs they advance for this claim is that, through careful geological research and investigation, it has become clear and evident to us that the existence of the plants preceded that of the animals, and that the existence of the animals preceded that of man. They hold, moreover, that both vegetable and animal kingdoms have undergone transformation; for in certain strata of the earth, plants have been discovered which existed in the past but which have since disappeared, meaning that they evolved, became hardier, and changed in form and appearance, and thus the species have changed. Likewise, in the strata of the earth there are certain animal species which have changed and altered. One of these is the snake, which has vestigial limbs, that is, signs indicating that it once had feet, which have disappeared over time and left behind only a remnant. In like manner, there is in man's vertebral column a vestige indicating that like other animals he once had a tail, of which, they assert, traces still remain. At one point that member was useful, but as man evolved, it lost its utility and hence it gradually disappeared. Likewise, as snakes came to live beneath the ground and became creeping animals, they were no longer in need of feet and so the latter disappeared, leaving behind a remnant. Their

principal proof is that these vestigial limbs are evidence of the existence of earlier limbs that have gradually disappeared for want of use,
and that they no longer have any benefit or reason to exist. Thus, the
fit and necessary limbs have remained, while the unnecessary ones
have gradually disappeared as a result of the transformation of the
species, but have left behind a remnant.

The first answer to this argument is that the antecedence of animals to man is not a proof that the essence of the human species was
altered or transformed or that man came from the animal kingdom.
For so long as it is acknowledged that these different beings have
appeared in time, it is possible that man simply came into existence
after the animal. Thus we observe in the vegetable kingdom that the
fruits of different trees do not appear all at once; on the contrary,
some appear earlier in the season and others later. This priority is not
a proof that the later fruit of one tree was produced from the earlier
fruit of another.

Secondly, these minor traces and vestigial limbs might have
some great underlying wisdom which the human mind has so far
been unable to fathom. How many things are found in this world
whose underlying wisdom to this day has not been grasped! Thus,
it is said in physiology—the science of the relations of the body's
organs—that the underlying wisdom and cause of the differences in
the colouration of animals and of human hair, or of the redness of
the lips, or of the variety of the colours of birds, are still unknown
and remain hidden and concealed. But it has been discovered that
the blackness of the pupil of the eye is due to its absorbing the rays of
the sun, for if it were of another colour—say, uniformly white—it
would not absorb these rays. Now, so long as the wisdom underlying
the things that we have mentioned is unknown, one may well imag-
ine that the reason and wisdom of the vestigial limbs, whether in the

animal or in man, is also unknown. Such an underlying wisdom of course exists, even though it may not be known.

Thirdly, even if we were to suppose that certain animals, or even man, once possessed limbs which have now disappeared, this would not be a sufficient proof of the transformation of the species. For man, from the conception of the embryo until the attainment of maturity, assumes different forms and appearances. His appearance, form, features, and colour change; that is, he passes from form to form and from appearance to appearance. Yet, from the formation of the embryo he belongs to the human species; that is, it is the embryo of a man and not of an animal. But at first this fact is not apparent; only later does it become plain and visible.

For example, let us suppose that man once bore a resemblance to the animal and that he has since evolved and transformed. Accepting this statement does not prove the transformation of species, but could instead be likened to the changes and transformations that the human embryo undergoes before reaching its full development and maturity, as was earlier mentioned. To be more explicit, let us suppose that man once walked on all fours or had a tail: This change and transformation is similar to that of the fetus in the womb of the mother. Even though the fetus develops and evolves in every possible way before it reaches its full development, from the beginning it belongs to a distinct species. The same holds true in the vegetable kingdom, where we observe that the original and distinctive character of the species does not change, while its form, colour, and mass do change, transform, and evolve.

To summarize: Just as man progresses, evolves, and is transformed from one form and appearance to another in the womb of the mother, while remaining from the beginning a human embryo, so too has man remained a distinct essence—that is, the human species—from the beginning of his formation in the matrix of the world, and has passed gradually from form to form. It follows that this change of appearance, this evolution of organs, and this growth and development do not preclude the originality of the species. Now, even accepting the reality of evolution and progress, nevertheless, from the moment of his appearance man has possessed perfect composition, and has had the capacity and potential to acquire both material and spiritual perfections and to become the embodiment of the verse, "Let Us make man in Our image, after Our likeness." At most, he has become more pleasing, more refined and graceful, and by virtue of civilization he has emerged from his wild state, just as the wild fruits become finer and sweeter under the cultivation of the gardener, and acquire ever greater delicacy and vitality.

The gardeners of the world of humanity are the Prophets of God. ('Abdu'l-Bahá, *Some Answered Questions*, no. 49)

. . . man is a reality which stands between light and darkness. From this standpoint his nature is threefold: animal, human and divine. The animal nature is darkness; the heavenly is light in light. ('Abdu'l-Bahá, *The Promulgation of Universal Peace*, p. 656)

In this world things live and die, and live again in other forms of life, but in the world of the spirit it is quite otherwise. The soul does not evolve from degree to degree as a law—it only evolves nearer to God, by the Mercy and Bounty of God. ('Abdu'l-Bahá, *Paris Talks*, no. 20.14)

All other beings are captives of nature and cannot free themselves from its exigencies: Man alone can withstand nature. So nature attracts all bodies to the centre of the earth, but through mechanical means man moves away from it and soars in the air; nature prevents man from crossing the sea, but man builds ships and traverses the heart of the great ocean, and so forth—the subject is endless. ('Abdu'l-Bahá, *Some Answered Questions*, no. 48.10)

It is evident and manifest that man is capable of breaking nature's laws. How does he accomplish it? Through a spirit with which God has endowed him at creation. This is a proof that the spirit of man differentiates and distinguishes him above all the lower kingdoms. It is this spirit to which the verse in the Old Testament refers when it states, "And God said, Let us make man in our image, after our likeness." The spirit of man alone penetrates the realities of God and partakes of the divine bounties. ('Abdu'l-Bahá, *The Promulgation of Universal Peace*, p. 361)

But the Essence of Divinity, the Sun of Truth, shines forth upon all horizons and is spreading its rays upon all things. Each creature is the recipient of some portion of that power, and man, who contains the perfection of the mineral, the vegetable and animal, as well as his own distinctive qualities, has become the noblest of created beings. It stands written that he is made in the Image of God. Mysteries that were hidden he discovers; and secrets that were concealed he brings into the light. By Science and by Art he brings hidden powers into the region of the visible world. Man perceives the hidden law in created things and co-operates with it. ('Abdu'l-Bahá, *'Abdu'l-Bahá in London*, p. 23)

Man alone has freedom, and, by his understanding or intellect, has been able to gain control of and adapt some of those natural laws to his own needs. By the power of his intellect he has discovered means by which he not only traverses great continents in express trains and crosses vast oceans in ships, but, like the fish he travels under water in submarines, and, imitating the birds, he flies through the air in airships. ('Abdu'l-Bahá, *Paris Talks*, no. 11.6)

Man is the sovereign of nature; he breaks nature's laws. . . . Man is gifted with a power whereby he penetrates and discovers the laws of nature, brings them forth from the world of invisibility into the plane of visibility. ('Abdu'l-Bahá, *The Promulgation of Universal Peace*, p. 361)

Man is able to resist and oppose nature inasmuch as he discovers the natures of things and, by virtue of this discovery, has mastery over nature itself. Indeed, all the crafts that man has devised proceed from this discovery. For example, he has invented the telegraph, which connects the East and the West. It is therefore evident that man rules over nature. ('Abdu'l-Bahá, *Some Answered Questions*, no. 1.4)

Although it is necessary for man to strive for material needs and comforts, his real need is the acquisition of the bounties of God. If he is bereft of divine bounties, spiritual susceptibilities and heavenly glad tidings, the life of man in this world has not yielded any worthy fruit. ('Abdu'l-Bahá, *The Promulgation of Universal Peace*, p. 475)

God has conferred upon man the gift of guidance, and in thankfulness for this great gift certain deeds must emanate from him. To express his gratitude for the favors of God man must show forth praiseworthy actions. In response to these bestowals he must render good deeds, be self-sacrificing, loving the servants of God, forfeiting even life for them, showing kindness to all the creatures. ('Abdu'l-Bahá, *The Promulgation of Universal Peace*, p. 330)

SCIENCE

We have permitted you to read such sciences as are profitable unto you, not such as end in idle disputation; better is this for you, if ye be of them that comprehend. (Bahá'u'lláh, *The Kitáb-i-Aqdas*, ¶77)

What bounty greater than this that science should be considered as an act of worship and art as service to the Kingdom of God. ('Abdu'l-Bahá, *Selections from the Writings of 'Abdu'l-Bahá*, no. 126.1)

We may think of science as one wing and religion as the other; a bird needs two wings for flight, one alone would be useless. Any religion that contradicts science or that is opposed to it, is only ignorance— for ignorance is the opposite of knowledge. Religion which consists only of rites and ceremonies of prejudice is not the truth. Let us earnestly endeavor to be the means of uniting religion and science. ('Abdu'l-Bahá, *Paris Talks*, no. 40.15)

God made religion and science to be the measure, as it were, of our understanding. Take heed that you neglect not such a wonderful power. Weigh all things in this balance. . . . Put all your beliefs into harmony with science; there can be no opposition, for truth is one. ('Abdu'l-Bahá, *Paris Talks*, no. 44.21)

Study the sciences, acquire more and more knowledge. Assuredly one may learn to the end of one's life! ('Abdu'l-Bahá, *Paris Talks*, no. 11.13)

All created things are captives of nature and subject to its laws. They cannot transgress the control of these laws in one detail or particular. . . . But man through the exercise of his scientific, intellectual power can rise out of this condition, can modify, change and control nature according to his own wishes and uses. Science, so to speak, is the breaker of the laws of nature. ('Abdu'l-Bahá, *The Promulgation of Universal Peace*, p. 40)

The first sign of the coming of age of humanity referred to in the Writings of Bahá'u'lláh is the emergence of a science which is described as that divine philosophy which will include the discovery of a radical approach to the transmutation of elements. This is an indication of the splendors of the future stupendous expansion of knowledge. (The Universal House of Justice, *The Kitáb-i-Aqdas*, Notes, no. 194)

World order can be founded only on an unshakable consciousness of the oneness of mankind, a spiritual truth which all the human sciences confirm. Anthropology, physiology, psychology, recognize only one human species, albeit infinitely varied in the secondary aspects of life. Recognition of this truth requires abandonment of prejudice—prejudice of every kind—race, class, color, creed, nation, sex, degree of material civilization, everything which enables people to consider themselves superior to others. (The Universal House of Justice, *The Promise of World Peace*, 1985, To the Peoples of the World)

Given that the question of climate change gives rise to social, economic, and environmental concerns across the world, interested Bahá'ís and Bahá'í institutions and agencies have naturally addressed it, whether at local, regional, national, or international levels. However, this does not mean that conclusions about scientific findings on climate change associated with such initiatives should be construed or presented as matters of religious conviction or obligation. (From a letter written on behalf of the Universal House of Justice, dated 29 November 2017, to three individuals)

Among the Bahá'í teachings are those concerning the importance of science. Great indeed is the claim of scientists . . . on the peoples of the world," Bahá'u'lláh observed. 'Abdu'l-Bahá wrote that the "sciences of today are bridges to reality" and repeatedly emphasized that "religion must be in conformity with science and reason." Significantly, on an occasion when a scientific question was asked of Shoghi Effendi, he responded in a letter written on his behalf that "we are a religion and not qualified to pass on scientific matters." And in reply to scientific issues raised on a number of occasions, he consistently advised Bahá'ís that such matters would need to be investigated by scientists. . . . Scientific inquiry into the question of human contributions to global warming has gradually unfolded over a century of investigation and, more recently, with intense scrutiny. While there will naturally be differences of view among individual scientists, there does exist at present a striking degree of agreement among experts in relevant fields about the cause and impact of climate change. Sound scientific results, obtained through the employment of sound scientific methods, produce knowledge that can be acted upon; ultimately, the outcomes of action must stand the test of further scientific inquiry and the objective facts of the physical world. In the spectrum of issues under discussion—which includes the extent of human contribution, projections of the possible future consequences, and alternatives for response—some aspects are, of course, less supported than others by scientific findings and hence subject to additional critical analysis. (From a letter written on behalf of the Universal House of Justice, dated 29 November 2017, to three individuals)

Reports appearing in the press and in scientific literature indicate that the study of the cloning of animals is at an early stage. Many fundamental questions about the biological and genetic features of this process, and its physiological implications, remain unresolved, and will only become clear with the passage of time. Nothing specific has been found in the Bahá'í Writings on the subject of human cloning. The House of Justice regards it as premature for it to give consideration to this matter and its spiritual consequences. For the present, the believers faced with questions about cloning are free to come to their own conclusions based on their knowledge of the Bahá'í teachings on the nature and purpose of life. However, they should be careful not to make dogmatic statements or to offer their own understanding as a teaching of the Faith. (From a letter written on behalf of the Universal House of Justice, dated 19 May 1998, to an individual, in Universal House of Justice, Research Department, *Reproduction and other Biological Subjects*)

Concern for justice protects the task of defining progress from the temptation to sacrifice the well-being of the generality of humankind—and even of the planet itself—to the advantages which technological breakthroughs can make available to privileged minorities. (*The Prosperity of Humankind*. A statement prepared by the Bahá'í International Community Office of Public Information, Haifa, 1995)

... despite the fact that most agricultural work in developing countries is carried out by low-income women, the primary shapers and users of agricultural technologies have been men. A key challenge is how to strengthen women's capacities to identify technological needs, and to create and adapt technologies in light of social needs and resource constraints. The empowerment of rural women and

130

their role in poverty and hunger eradication, development and current challenges. (Bahá'í International Community, Contribution to the 56th Session of the United Nations Commission on the Status of Women, New York, 27 February 2012)

The technologies and resources exist to meet the basic needs of humanity and to eliminate poverty. Equity in the use of these technologies and resources, however, will come about only with certain understandings and commitments. (Bahá'í International Community, "Valuing Spirituality in Development: Initial Considerations Regarding the Creation of Spiritually Based Indicators for Development." A concept paper written for the World Faiths and Development Dialogue, Lambeth Palace, London, 18–19 February 1998)

Such advances in science and technology were reciprocal in their effects. Grains of sand—the most humble and ostensibly worthless of materials—metamorphosed into silicon wafers and optically pure glass, making possible the creation of worldwide communications networks. This, together with the deployment of ever more sophisticated satellite systems, has begun providing access to the accumulated knowledge of the entire human race for people everywhere, without distinction. It is apparent that the decades immediately ahead will see the integration of telephone, television, and computer technologies into a single, unified system of communication and information, whose inexpensive appliances will be available on a mass scale. It would be difficult to exaggerate the psychological and social impact of the anticipated replacement of the jumble of existing monetary systems—for many, the ultimate fortress of nationalist pride—by a single world currency operating largely through electronic impulses." (Bahá'í International Community, "Who is Writing the Future," ¶22)

On an institutional level, a global entity with a strong scientific advisory capacity is needed to streamline reporting and decision-making processes, including the voices of non-state actors. It must coherently link environmental issues to social and economic priorities, for none of these can advance in isolation. (Bahá'í International Community, "Eradicating Poverty: Moving Forward as One," the Bahá'í International Community's Statement on Poverty, 14 February 2008)

AGRICULTURE AND THE COMMON GOOD

Again, is there any deed in the world that would be nobler than service to the common good? Is there any greater blessing conceivable for a man, than that he should become the cause of the education, the development, the prosperity and honor of his fellow-creatures? ('Abdu'l-Bahá, *The Secret of Divine Civilization,* ¶132)

One of the most important principles of the Teaching of Bahá'u'lláh is:

The right of every human being to the daily bread whereby they exist, or the equalization of the means of livelihood. ('Abdu'l-Bahá, *Paris Talks,* no. 46.1–2)

God is not partial and is no respecter of persons. He has made provision for all. The harvest comes forth for everyone. The rain showers upon everybody and the heat of the sun is destined to warm everyone. The verdure of the earth is for everyone. Therefore, there should be for all humanity the utmost happiness, the utmost comfort, the utmost well-being. But if conditions are such that some are happy and comfortable and some in misery, some are accumulating exorbitant wealth and others are in dire want—under such a system it is impossible for man to be happy and impossible for him to win the good pleasure of God. God is kind to all. The good pleasure of

God consists in the welfare of all the individual members of mankind. ('Abdu'l-Bahá, *The Promulgation of Universal Peace*, p. 439)

As to your fourth question, Shoghi Effendi believes that it is preferable not to confuse the methods explained by the Master with present systems. They may have many resemblances but also many points of difference. Moreover these general statements we have in the teachings have to be explained and applied by the House of Justice before we can really appreciate their significance. (From a letter written on behalf of Shoghi Effendi, dated 21 October 1932, in Universal House of Justice, Research Department, *Extracts from the Bahá'í Writings on the Subject of Agriculture and Related Subjects*, revised 12 November 2001)

The crisis that exists in the world is not confined to farmers. Its effects have reached every means of livelihood. The farmers are in a sense better off because they at least have food to eat. But on the whole the crisis is serving a great purpose. It is broadening the outlook of man, teaching him to think internationally, forcing him to take into consideration the welfare of his neighbours if he wishes to improve his own condition. In short it is forcing humanity to appreciate the significance of and follow the precepts laid by Bahá'u'lláh. (From a letter written on behalf of Shoghi Effendi, dated 2 March 1932, to an individual, in Universal House of Justice, Research Department, *Agriculture and Rural Life*, 1995)

As the work of community building intensifies, the friends are using the new capacities they have developed to improve conditions in the society around them, their enthusiasm kindled by their study of the divine teachings. Short-term projects have soared in number, formal programmes have expanded their reach, and there are now more Bahá'í-inspired development organizations engaged in education, health, agriculture, and other areas. (The Universal House of Justice, Riḍván 2018, to the Bahá'ís of the World)

The Office of Social and Economic Development was established at the Bahá'í World Centre to assist us in promoting and coordinating the activities of the friends worldwide. Bahá'í activities for social and economic development, at whatever level of complexity, were at that time counted in the hundreds. Today they number in the tens of thousands, including hundreds of sustained projects such as schools and scores of development organizations. The broad range of current activities spans efforts from villages and neighborhoods to regions and nations, addressing an array of challenges, including education from preschool to university, literacy, health, the environment, support for refugees, advancement of women, empowerment of junior youth, elimination of racial prejudice, agriculture, local economies, and village development. The society-building power of Bahá'u'lláh's Cause has begun to be more systematically expressed in the collective life of the friends as a result of the acceleration of the process of expansion and consolidation, especially in advanced clusters. Beyond this, of course, countless believers, through their professional and voluntary efforts, contribute their energies and insights to projects and organizations established for the common good. (The Universal House of Justice, message dated 9 November 2018, to the Bahá'ís of the World)

The Bahá'í teachings affirm the spiritual bond which binds the human being to the land whence he has come, and seek to create a way of life in which each individual can find within himself a sense of harmony with the natural forces of the physical world. We feel that rural development is best accomplished through inculcation of some fundamental values and attitudes to animate and orient each member of society. It is essential, for instance, that the dignity of work be emphasized, and that manual work be regarded as no less meritorious than other forms of work when performed with the attitude of service to the common welfare. Agriculture is the foundation of a sound economic system, as it is the means by which the most basic human physical needs for survival are met; a change in values to accord agriculture its proper position in the scale of occupations would increase its attraction to the new generation and diminish the tendency to depopulate the countryside and overcrowd the cities. (Bahá'í International Community, "Spiritual and Social Values for Rural Development." Paper presented to the Twentieth Conference of the South Pacific Commission Port Moresby, Papua New Guinea, 18 October 1980)

Issues of food, nutrition, health and shelter are central to the challenge of providing an adequate standard of living for all members of the human family. These issues cannot, however, be tackled solely as technical or economic problems. Eliminating hunger and malnutrition; establishing food security; providing adequate shelter; and achieving health for all will require a shift in values, a commitment to equity, and a corresponding reorientation of policies, goals and programs. . . . The economics of food production and distribution will have to be reoriented and the critical role of the farmer in food and economic security properly valued. With regard to health—the physical, spiritual, mental and social well-being of the individual—access to clean water, shelter, and some form of cheap energy would go a long way toward eradicating the problems that currently plague vast numbers of individuals and communities. It must be acknowledged, however, that some illnesses reflect unwholesome human behavior. The inclusion of moral development in education would, therefore, help to reduce significantly certain current health problems. (Bahá'í International Community, "Valuing Spirituality in Development: Initial Considerations Regarding the Creation of Spiritually Based Indicators for Development." A concept paper written for the World Faiths and Development Dialogue, Lambeth Palace, London, 18–19 February 1998)

A core element of a strategy of sustainable development is the reform of agricultural policies and processes. Food production and agriculture is the world's single largest source of employment, nearly 70% of the poor in developing countries live in rural areas and depend on agriculture for their livelihoods. Although farming has been devalued by manufacturing and a rapidly expanding urban population, agriculture still represents the fundamental basis of economic and community life: malnourishment and food insecurity suffocate all attempts at development progress. (Bahá'í International Community, "Eradicating Poverty: Moving Forward as One," the Bahá'í International Community's Statement on Poverty, 14 February 2008)

Food as Sustenance

Should a man wish to adorn himself with the ornaments of the earth, to wear its apparels, or partake of the benefits it can bestow, no harm can befall him, if he alloweth nothing whatever to intervene between him and God, for God hath ordained every good thing, whether created in the heavens or in the earth, for such of His servants as truly believe in Him. Eat ye, O people, of the good things which God hath allowed you, and deprive not yourselves from His wondrous bounties. Render thanks and praise unto Him, and be of them that are truly thankful. (Bahá'u'lláh, *Gleanings from the Writings of Bahá'u'lláh*, no. 128.4)

In all circumstances they should conduct themselves with moderation; if the meal be only one course this is more pleasing in the sight of God; however, according to their means, they should seek to have this single dish be of good quality. (Bahá'u'lláh, in *Lights of Guidance*, no. 1004)

What will be the food of the future? Fruit and grains. The time will come when meat will no longer be eaten. Medical science is only in its infancy, yet it has shown that our natural diet is that which grows out of the ground. The people will gradually develop up to the condition of this natural food. ('Abdu'l-Bahá, cited in Julia M. Grundy, *Ten Days in the Light of 'Akká*, pp. 8–9, in *Lights of Guidance*, no. 1009)

The child must, from the day of his birth, be provided with whatever is conducive to his health and know ye this: so far as possible, the mother's milk is best for, more agreeable and better suited to the child, unless she should fall ill or her milk should run entirely dry. ('Abdu'l-Bahá, Tablet to an individual, in *Lights of Guidance*, no. 1005)

Food as Medicine

Do not neglect medical treatment when it is necessary, but leave it off when health has been restored. . . . Treat disease through diet, by preference, refraining from the use of drugs; and if you find what is required in a single herb, do not resort to a compounded medicament. Abstain from drugs when the health is good, but administer them when necessary. (Bahá'u'lláh, cited in J. E. Esslemont, *Bahá'u'lláh and the New Era*, p.106)

It is certain that in this wonderful new age the development of medical science will lead to the doctors' healing their patients

137

with foods. For the sense of sight, the sense of hearing, of taste, of smell, of touch—all these are discriminative faculties, their purpose being to separate the beneficial from whatever causeth harm. . . . ('Abdu'l-Bahá, *Selections from the Writings of 'Abdu'l-Bahá,* no. 134.9)

The Báb hath said that the people of Bahá must develop the science of medicine to such a high degree that they will heal illnesses by means of foods. The basic reason for this is that if, in some component substance of the human body, an imbalance should occur, altering its correct, relative proportion to the whole, this fact will inevitably result in the onset of disease. If, for example, the starch component should be unduly augmented, or the sugar component decreased, an illness will take control. It is the function of a skilled physician to determine which constituent of his patient's body hath suffered diminution, which hath been augmented. Once he hath discovered this, he must prescribe a food containing the diminished element in considerable amounts, to reestablish the body's essential equilibrium. The patient, once his constitution is again in balance, will be rid of his disease. ('Abdu'l-Bahá, *Selections from the Writings of 'Abdu'l-Bahá,* no. 134.6)

. . . other animals have never studied medical science, nor carried on researches into diseases or medicines, treatments or cures—even so, when one of them falleth a prey to sickness, nature leadeth it, in fields or desert places, to the very plant which, once eaten, will rid the animal of its disease. ('Abdu'l-Bahá, *Selections from the Writings of 'Abdu'l-Bahá,* no. 134.7)

. . . man hath perversely continued to serve his lustful appetites, and he would not content himself with simple foods. Rather, he prepared for himself food that was compounded of many ingredients, of substances differing one from the other. With this, and with the perpetrating of vile and ignoble acts, his attention was engrossed, and he abandoned the temperance and moderation of a natural way of life. The result was the engendering of diseases both violent and diverse. . . .

The outer, physical causal factor in disease, however, is a disturbance in the balance, the proportionate equilibrium of all those elements of which the human body is composed. To illustrate: the body of man is a compound of many constituent substances, each component being present in a prescribed amount, contributing to the essential equilibrium of the whole. So long as these constituents remain in their due proportion, according to the natural balance of the whole—that is, no component suffereth a change in its natural proportionate degree and balance, no component being either augmented or decreased—there will be no physical cause for the incursion of disease. . . . ('Abdu'l-Bahá, *Selections from the Writings of 'Abdu'l-Bahá*, no. 134.2–3)

One day he came to me and complained of a chronic ailment. "I have suffered from chills and fever for two years," he said. "The doctors have prescribed a purgative, and quinine. The fever stops a few days; then it returns. They give me more quinine, but still the fever returns. I am weary of this life, and can no longer do my work. Save me!"

"What food would you most enjoy?" I asked him. "What would you eat with great appetite?"

"I don't know," he said.

Jokingly, I named off the different dishes. When I came to barley soup with whey (ásh-i-kashk), he said, "Very good! But on condition there is braised garlic in it."

I directed them to prepare this for him, and I left. The next day he presented himself and told me: "I ate a whole bowlful of the soup. Then I laid my head on my pillow and slept peacefully till morning."

In short, from then on he was perfectly well for about two years. One day a believer came to me and said: "Muḥammad-Hádí is burning up with fever." I hurried to his bedside and found him with a fever of 42° Centigrade. He was barely conscious. "What has he done?" I asked. "When he became feverish," was the reply, "he said that he knew from experience what he should do. Then he ate his fill of barley soup with whey and braised garlic; and this was the result."

I was astounded at the workings of fate. I told them: "Because, two years ago, he had been thoroughly purged and his system was clear; because he had a hearty appetite for it, and his ailment was fever and chills, I prescribed the barley soup. But this time, with the different foods he has had, with no appetite, and especially with a high fever, there was no reason to diagnose the previous chronic condition. How could he have eaten the soup!" They answered, "It was fate." Things had gone too far; Muḥammad-Hádí was past saving. ('Abdu'l-Bahá, *Memorials of the Faithful,* no. 25)

Now we will speak of material healing. The science of medicine is still in its infancy and has not yet reached maturity. But when it reaches that stage, treatments will be administered with things that are not repulsive to the senses of taste and smell, that is, through foods, fruits, and plants that have an agreeable taste and a pleasant smell. For the cause of the intrusion of illness into the human body is either a physical agent or a nervous excitement and stimulation. As to physical agents, which are the primary cause of illness, their effect is due to the following: The human body is composed of numerous elements according to a particular state of equilibrium. So long as this equilibrium is maintained, man is preserved from sickness, but should this fundamental balance, which is the central requirement of a sound constitution, be upset, the constitution will be disrupted and illnesses will supervene. ('Abdu'l-Bahá, *Some Answered Questions,* no. 73.2)

In the Kitáb-i-Aqdas Bahá'u'lláh has stated: "Whenever ye fall ill, refer to competent physicians." . . .

In matters of diet, as in medicine, the Universal House of Justice feels that the believers should be aware that a huge body of scientific knowledge has been accumulated as a guide to our habits and practices. Here too, as in all other things, the believers should be conscious of the two principles of moderation and courtesy in the way they express their opinions and in deciding whether they should refuse food offered to them or request special foods. There are, of course, instances where a believer would be fully justified in abstaining from or eating only certain foods for some medical reason, but this is a different matter and would be understood by any reasonable person. (From a letter written on behalf of the Universal House of Justice, dated 24 January 1977, to an individual believer)

No specific school of nutrition or medicine has been associated with the Bahá'í teachings. . . . Moreover, in this connection the Guardian's secretary has stated on his behalf that "It is premature to try and elaborate on the few general references to health and medicine made in our Holy Scriptures." The believers must guard against seizing upon any particular text which may appeal to them and which they may only partially or even incorrectly understand. . . . (From a letter written on behalf of the Universal House of Justice, dated 24 January 1977, to an individual believer)

Dear Bahá'í Friend,
Your email of 14 December 1999, inquiring about a translation of Bahá'u'lláh's Tablet to a Physician subsequent to the one found in Bahá'u'lláh and the New Era, was received by the Universal House of Justice and referred to our Department for reply.

Excerpts from Bahá'u'lláh's Tablet to a Physician appeared in Star of the West, volume 13, page 252, as well as in many and various Bahá'í newsletters and compilations, as an early translation of a portion of the Tablet entitled "Lawḥ-i-Ṭibb," revealed by Bahá'u'lláh in honour of Mírzá Muḥammad Riḍá Yazdí, a physician. However, until such time as conditions are propitious for the Tablet to be translated, only portions of it have an authorized translation. For your convenience, we are enclosing the text of the early, partial translation of the Tablet to a Physician which was published in Star of the West, as cited above, along with a related exhortation from Bahá'u'lláh taken from Star of the West, volume 21, number 5, page 160. Furthermore, it may interest you to know that the prayer starting with the words, "Thy Name is my healing . . ." is also found in this Tablet.

With regard to the Tablet, on 18 December 1945 a letter was written on behalf of the beloved Guardian to an individual believer stating:

"The Tablet to a Physician was addressed to a man who was a student of the old type of healing prevalent in the East and familiar with the terminology used in those days, and He addresses him in terms used by the medical men of those days. These terms are quite different from those used by modern medicine, and one would have to have a deep knowledge of this former school of medicine to understand the questions Bahá'u'lláh was elucidating. . . ."

Enclosure:

Physical Healing

Some rules for health, from a Tablet revealed by Bahá'u'lláh.

O God! The Supreme Knower! The Ancient Tongue speaks that which will satisfy the wise in the absence of doctors.

O People, do not eat except when you are hungry. Do not drink after you have retired to sleep.

Exercise is good when the stomach is empty; it strengthens the muscles. When the stomach is full it is very harmful.

Do not neglect medical treatment, when it is necessary, but leave it off when the body is in good condition.

Do not take nourishment except when (the process of) digestion is completed. Do not swallow until you have thoroughly masticated your food.

Treat disease first of all through diet, and refrain from medicine. If you can find what you need for healing in a single herb do not use a compound medicine. Leave off medicine when the health is good, and use it in case of necessity.

If two diametrically opposite foods are put on the table do not mix them. Be content with one of them. Take first the liquid food before partaking of solid food. The taking of food before that which you have already eaten is digested is dangerous. . . .

When you have eaten walk a little that the food may settle.

That which is difficult to masticate is forbidden by the wise. Thus the Supreme Pen commands you.

A light meal in the morning is as a light to the body.

Avoid all harmful habits: they cause unhappiness in the world.

Search for the causes of disease. This saying is the conclusion of this utterance.
(Star of the West, vol. 13, no. 9, December 1922, p. 252)

In God must be our trust. There is no God but Him, the Healer, the Knower, the Helper. . . . Nothing in earth or heaven is outside the grasp of God.

O doctor! In treating the sick, first mention the name of God, the Possessor of the Day of Judgment, and then use what God hath destined for the healing of His creatures. By My Life! The doctor who has drunk from the Wine of My Love, his visit is healing, and his breath is mercy and hope. Cling to him for the welfare of the constitution. He is confirmed by God in his treatment. (Star of the West, vol. 21, no. 5, August 1930, p. 160)
(From a letter written on behalf of the Universal House of Justice, dated 2 April 2000, to an individual)

Animals as Food

As humanity progresses, meat will be used less and less, for the teeth of man are not carnivorous. For example, the lion is endowed with carnivorous teeth, which are intended for meat, and if meat be not found, the lion starves. The lion cannot graze; its teeth are of different shape. . . . The domestic animals have herbivorous teeth formed to cut grass, which is their fodder. The human teeth, the molars, are formed to grind grain. The front teeth, the incisors, are for fruits, etc. It is, therefore, quite apparent according to the implements for eating that man's food is intended to be grain and not meat. When mankind is more fully developed, the eating of meat will gradually cease. ('Abdu'l-Bahá, *The Promulgation of Universal Peace*, p. 236)

All the teeth of man are made for eating fruit, cereals, and vegetables. These four teeth, however, are designed for breaking hard shells, such as those of almonds. But eating meat is not forbidden or unlawful, nay, the point is this, that it is possible for man to live without eating meat and still be strong. Meat is nourishing and containeth the elements of herbs, seeds, and fruits; therefore sometimes it is essential for the sick and for the rehabilitation of health. There is no objection in the Law of God to the eating of meat if it is required. So if thy constitution is rather weak and thou findest meat useful, thou mayest eat it. ('Abdu'l-Bahá, from a Tablet to an individual, *Compilation of Compilations*, Vol. 1, p. 463)

Some of the teeth of man are like millstones to grind the grain, and some are sharp to cut the fruit. Therefore he is not in need of meat, nor is he obliged to eat it. Even without eating meat he would live with the utmost vigour and energy. For example, the community of the Brahmins in India do not eat meat; notwithstanding this they are not inferior to other nations in strength, power, vigour, outward senses or intellectual virtues. Truly, the killing of animals and the eating of their meat is somewhat contrary to pity and compassion, and if one can content oneself with cereals, fruit, oil and nuts, such as pistachios, almonds and so on, it would undoubtedly be better and more pleasing. ('Abdu'l-Bahá, from a Tablet to an individual, *Compilation of Compilations*, Vol. 1, p. 463)

In regard to the question as to whether people ought to kill animals for food or not, there is no explicit statement in the Bahá'í Sacred

Scriptures (as far as I know) in favour or against it. It is certain, however, that if man can live on a purely vegetarian diet and thus avoid killing animals, it would be much preferable. This is, however, a very controversial question and the Bahá'ís are free to express their views on it. (From a letter written on behalf of Shoghi Effendi, dated 9 July 1931, to an individual believer, in *Compilation of Compilations*, Vol. 1, p. 462)

The eating of pork is not forbidden in the Bahá'í Teachings. (From a letter written on behalf of Shoghi Effendi, dated 27 March 1938, to an individual believer, in *Compilation of Compilations*, Vol. 1, p. 54)

. . . you particularly ask about references in the Old Testament as they relate to meat and fish, the House of Justice has asked us to quote for you the following excerpt taken from a letter written on behalf of the beloved Guardian by his secretary to an individual believer: ". . . there is nothing in the teachings about whether people should eat their food cooked or raw; exercise or not exercise; resort to specific therapies or not; nor is it forbidden to eat meat." (From a letter written on behalf of the Universal House of Justice, dated 19 June 1977, to an individual believer, in *Compilation of Compilations*, Vol. 1, p. 85)

As in so many other areas, the Teachings of Bahá'u'lláh in this regard follow the golden mean: kindness toward animals is definitely upheld, vegetarianism is encouraged, hunting is regulated, but certain latitude is left to individual conscience and in practical regard to the diversity of circumstances under which human beings live. For example, the indigenous peoples of the Arctic would be hard-pressed to subsist without recourse to animal products. (From a letter written on behalf of the Universal House of Justice, dated 20 November 1992, to an individual)

"Your concern for the prevention of cruelty to animals and for restraint in exploiting them unduly for food and other purposes is indeed praiseworthy; however, the House of Justice is not aware of any absolute prohibition in any Holy Book against the use of animals for food and clothing. As the laws brought by Bahá'u'lláh become known and operative throughout the world, we believe that humanity will find the proper balance in adjusting itself to nature and to the world of animals. (From a letter written on behalf of the Universal House of Justice, dated 16 December 1998, to an individual)

Admonitions Regarding Health
Take heed lest, when partaking of food, ye plunge your hands into the contents of bowls and platters. (Bahá'u'lláh, The Kitáb-i-Aqdas, ¶46)

Wash ye every soiled thing with water that hath undergone no alteration in any one of the three respects The *"three respects"* referred to in this verse are changes in the color, taste or smell of the water. (Bahá'u'lláh, The Kitáb-i-Aqdas, ¶74)

Question: Concerning pure water, and the point at which it is considered used.
Answer: Small quantities of water, such as one cupful, or even two or three, must be considered used after a single washing of the face and hands. But a kurr or more of water remaineth unchanged after one or two washings of the face, and there is no objection to its use unless

it is altered in one of the three ways, for example its color is changed, in which case it should be looked upon as used. (Bahá'u'lláh, *The Kitáb-i-Aqdas,* Questions and Answers, p. 212, Q 91)

Beware of using any substance that induceth sluggishness and torpor in the human temple and inflicteth harm upon the body. (Bahá'u'lláh, The Kitáb-i-Aqdas, ¶155)

This prohibition of the use of opium is reiterated by Bahá'u'lláh in the final paragraph of the Kitáb-i-Aqdas. In this connection, Shoghi Effendi stated that one of the requirements for "a chaste and holy life" is "total abstinence . . . from opium, and from similar habit-forming drugs." Heroin, hashish and other derivatives of cannabis such as marijuana, as well as hallucinogenic agents such as LSD, peyote and similar substances, are regarded as falling under this prohibition.

'Abdu'l-Bahá has written:

> As to opium, it is foul and accursed. God protect us from the punishment He inflicteth on the user. According to the explicit Text of the Most Holy Book, it is forbidden, and its use is utterly condemned. Reason showeth that smoking opium is a kind of insanity, and experience attesteth that the user is completely cut off from the human kingdom. May God protect all against the perpetration of an act so hideous as this, an act which layeth in ruins the very foundation of what it is to be human, and which causeth the user to be dispossessed for ever and ever. For opium fasteneth on the soul so that the user's conscience dieth, his mind is blotted away, his perceptions are eroded. It turneth the living into the dead. It quencheth the natural heat. No greater harm can be conceived than that which opium inflicteth. Fortunate are they who never

even speak the name of it; then think how wretched is the user.
O ye lovers of God! In this, the cycle of Almighty God, violence
and force, constraint and oppression, are one and all condemned.
It is, however, mandatory that the use of opium be prevented by
any means whatsoever, that perchance the human race may be
delivered from this most powerful of plagues. And otherwise, woe
and misery to whoso falleth short of his duty to his Lord.

In one of His Tablets 'Abdu'l-Bahá has stated concerning opium:
"the user, the buyer and the seller are all deprived of the bounty and
grace of God."

In yet another Tablet, 'Abdu'l-Bahá has written:

Regarding hashish you have pointed out that some Persians have
become habituated to its use. Gracious God! This is the worst of
all intoxicants, and its prohibition is explicitly revealed. Its use
causeth the disintegration of thought and the complete torpor of the
soul. How could anyone seek the fruit of the infernal tree, and by
partaking of it, be led to exemplify the qualities of a monster? How
could one use this forbidden drug, and thus deprive himself of the
blessings of the All-Merciful?

Alcohol consumeth the mind and causeth man to commit acts of
absurdity, but this opium, this foul fruit of the infernal tree, and
this wicked hashish extinguish the mind, freeze the spirit, petrify
the soul, waste the body and leave man frustrated and lost.

It should be noted that the above prohibition against taking certain
classes of drugs does not forbid their use when prescribed by qualified physicians as part of a medical treatment. (The Universal House
of Justice, *The Kitáb-i-Aqdas,* Notes, no. 170)

In one of His Tablets, Bahá'u'lláh states:

Beware lest ye exchange the Wine of God for your own wine, for it will stupefy your minds, and turn your faces away from the Countenance of God, the All-Glorious, the Peerless, the Inaccessible. Approach it not, for it hath been forbidden unto you by the behest of God, the Exalted, the Almighty. 'Abdu'l-Bahá *explains that the Aqdas prohibits "both light and strong drinks," and He states that the reason for prohibiting the use of alcoholic drinks is because "alcohol leadeth the mind astray and causeth the weakening of the body."*

Shoghi Effendi, in letters written on his behalf, states that this prohibition includes not only the consumption of wine but of "everything that deranges the mind," and he clarifies that the use of alcohol is permitted only when it constitutes part of a medical treatment which is implemented "under the advice of a competent and conscientious physician, who may have to prescribe it for the cure of some special ailment." (The Universal House of Justice, *The Kitáb-i-Aqdas*, Notes, no. 144)

O ye, God's loved ones! Experience hath shown how greatly the renouncing of smoking, of intoxicating drink, and of opium, conduceth to health and vigour, to the expansion and keenness of the mind and to bodily strength. There is today a people who strictly avoid tobacco, intoxicating liquor and opium. This people is far and away superior to the others, for strength and physical courage, for health, beauty and comeliness. A single one of their men can stand up to ten men of another tribe. This hath proved true of the entire people: that is, member for member, each individual of this community is in every respect superior to the individuals of other communities. Make ye then a mighty effort, that the purity and sanctity which, above all else, are cherished by 'Abdu'l-Bahá, shall distinguish the people of Bahá; that in every kind of excellence the people of God shall surpass all other human beings; that both outwardly and inwardly they shall prove superior to the rest; that for purity, immaculacy, refinement, and the preservation of health, they shall be leaders in the vanguard of those who know. And that by their freedom from enslavement, their knowledge, their self-control, they shall be first among the pure, the free and the wise. ('Abdu'l-Bahá, *Selections from the Writings of 'Abdu'l-Bahá*, no. 129.13)

With regard to the question you have raised in connection with the sale of alcoholic liquors by the friends: he wishes me to inform you that dealings with such liquors, in any form, are highly discouraged in the Cause. The believers should, therefore, consider it their spiritual obligation to refrain from undertaking any business enterprise that would involve them in the traffic of alcoholic drinks. (From a letter written on behalf of Shoghi Effendi, dated 6 November 1935, to a Local Spiritual Assembly, in *Compilation of Compilations*, vol. II, no. 1793)

'Abdu'l-Bahá, adding His voice to that of the Blessed Beauty, has written, "The drinking of wine is, according to the text of the Most Holy Book, forbidden; for it is the cause of chronic diseases, weakeneth the nerves, and consumeth the mind." He has also written, "Regarding the use of liquor, according to the text of the Book of Aqdas, both light and strong drinks are prohibited." He further states, "Intellect and the faculty of comprehension are God's gifts whereby man is distinguished from other animals. Will a wise man want to lose this Light in the darkness of intoxication? No, by God!" In answer to questions, Shoghi Effendi's elucidations, written on his behalf, provide further guidance on this subject. In these letters the habit of drinking is described as a "great misery" and a "great evil." (From a letter written on behalf of the Universal House of Justice, dated 30 March 1997, to all National Spiritual Assemblies in Africa)

PART 3

DEVELOPING THE DIVINE ECONOMY

The health of the planet and its citizens is dependent on vigilant stewardship of its physical and human resources. Consideration for the well-being of the farmer is central to the operation of an equitable economic system that safeguards the common good. Spiritual principles informing action in the material world can ensure justice in economic policy.

DEVELOPING THE
DIVINE ECONOMY

All men have been created to carry forward an ever-advancing civilization. (Bahá'u'lláh, *Gleanings from the Writings of Bahá'u'lláh*, no. 109.2)

The question of economics must commence with the farmer and then be extended to the other classes inasmuch as the number of farmers is greater than all other classes, many many times greater. Therefore, it is fitting that the economic problem be first solved with the farmer, for the farmer is the first active agent in the body politic. In brief, from among the wise men in every village a board should be organized and the affairs of that village should be under the control of that board. ('Abdu'l-Bahá, from a Tablet translated from the Persian, dated October 4, 1912, to an individual believer, in *Extracts from the Bahá'í Writings on the Subject of Agriculture and Related Subjects)*

The fundamentals of the whole economic condition are divine in nature and are associated with the world of the heart and spirit. This is fully explained in the Bahá'í teaching, and without knowledge of

155

its principles no improvement in the economic state can be realized. ('Abdu'l-Bahá, *The Promulgation of Universal Peace*, p. 334)

When the love of God is established, everything else will be realized. This is the true foundation of all economics. Reflect upon it. Endeavor to become the cause of the attraction of souls rather than to enforce minds. ('Abdu'l-Bahá, *The Promulgation of Universal Peace*, p. 334)

Bahá'u'lláh has given instructions regarding every one of the questions confronting humanity. He has given teachings and instructions with regard to every one of the problems with which man struggles. Among them are [the teachings] concerning the question of economics, that all the members of the body politic may enjoy through the working out of this solution the greatest happiness, welfare and comfort without any harm or injury attacking the general order of things. Thereby no difference or dissension will occur. No sedition or contention will take place. ('Abdu'l-Bahá, *The Promulgation of Universal Peace*, p. 437)

First and foremost is the principle that to all the members of the body politic shall be given the greatest achievements of the world of humanity. Each one shall have the utmost welfare and well-being. To solve this problem we must begin with the farmer; there will we lay a foundation for system and order because the peasant class and the agricultural class exceed other classes in the importance of their service. ('Abdu'l-Bahá, *The Promulgation of Universal Peace*, p. 437)

The degrees of society must be preserved. The farmer will continue to till the soil, the artist pursue his art, the banker to finance the nations. An army has need of its general, captain, and private soldiers.

The degrees varying with the pursuits are essential. But in this Bahá'í plan there is no class hatred: Each is to be protected and each individual member of the body politic is to live in the greatest comfort and happiness. Work is to be provided for all and there will be no needy ones seen in the streets. ('Abdu'l-Bahá, in *Star of the West*, vol. 22, no. 1, p. 3)

Would the status of ancient thought, the crudeness of arts and crafts, the insufficiency of scientific attainment serve us today? Would the agricultural methods of the ancients suffice in the twentieth century? Transportation in the former ages was restricted to conveyance by animals. How would it provide for human needs today? If modes of transportation had not been reformed, the teeming millions now upon the earth would die of starvation. Without the railway and the fast-going steamship, the world of the present day would be as dead. How could great cities such as New York and London subsist if dependent upon ancient means of conveyance? It is also true of other things which have been reformed in proportion to the needs of the present time. Had they not been reformed, man could not find subsistence. If these material tendencies are in such need of reformation, how much greater the need in the world of the human spirit, the world of human thought, perception, virtues and bounties! Is it possible that that need has remained stationary while the world has been advancing in every other condition and direction? It is impossible. ('Abdu'l-Bahá, *The Promulgation of Universal Peace*, p. 390)

In this day, however, means of communication have multiplied, and the five continents of the earth have virtually merged into one. . . . In like manner all the members of the human family, whether peoples or governments, cities or villages, have become increasingly interdependent. For none is self-sufficiency any longer possible, inasmuch as political ties unite all peoples and nations, and the bonds of trade and industry, of agriculture and education, are being strengthened every day. Hence the unity of all mankind can in this day be achieved. (Shoghi Effendi, *The World Order of Bahá'u'lláh*, p. 38)

"God," 'Abdu'l-Bahá Himself declares, *"maketh no distinction between the white and the black. If the hearts are pure both are acceptable unto Him. God is no respecter of persons on account of either color or race. All colors are acceptable unto Him, be they white, black, or yellow. Inasmuch as all were created in the image of God, we must bring ourselves to realize that all embody divine possibilities."* *"In the estimation of God,"* He states, *"all men are equal. There is no distinction or preference for any soul, in the realm of His justice and equity."* *"God did not make these divisions,"* He affirms; *"these divisions have had their origin in man himself. Therefore, as they are against the plan and purpose of God they are false and imaginary."* . . .

"This question of the union of the white and the black is very important," He warns, *"for if it is not realized, erelong great difficulties will arise, and harmful results will follow."* *"If this matter remaineth without change,"* is yet another warning, *"enmity will be increased day by day, and the final result will be hardship and may end in bloodshed."*

A tremendous effort is required by both races if their outlook, their manners, and conduct are to reflect, in this darkened age, the spirit and teachings of the Faith of Bahá'u'lláh. Casting away once and for all the fallacious doctrine of racial superiority, with all its attendant evils, confusion, and miseries, and welcoming and encouraging the intermixture of races, and tearing down the barriers that now divide them, they should each endeavor, day and night, to fulfill their particular responsibilities in the common task which so urgently faces them.

Let them, while each is attempting to contribute its share to the solution of this perplexing problem, call to mind the warnings of 'Abdu'l-Bahá, and visualize, while there is yet time, the dire consequences that must follow if this challenging and unhappy situation that faces the entire American nation is not definitely remedied. . . . Let neither think that the solution of so vast a problem is a matter that exclusively concerns the other. Let neither think that such a problem can either easily or immediately be resolved. Let neither think that they can wait confidently for the solution of this problem until the initiative has been taken, and the favorable circumstances created, by agencies that stand outside the orbit of their Faith. Let neither think that anything short of genuine love, extreme patience, true humility, consummate tact, sound initiative, mature wisdom, and deliberate, persistent, and prayerful effort, can succeed in blotting out the stain which this patent evil has left on the fair name of their common country. Let them rather believe, and be firmly convinced, that on their mutual understanding, their amity, and sustained cooperation, must depend, more than on any other force or organization operating outside the circle of their Faith, the deflection of that dangerous course so greatly feared by 'Abdu'l-Bahá, and the materialization of the hopes He cherished for their joint contribution to the fulfillment of that country's glorious destiny. (Shoghi Effendi, *Advent of Divine Justice*, ¶56–58)

The interdependence of the peoples and nations of the earth, whatever the leaders of the divisive forces of the world may say or do, is already an accomplished fact. Its unity in the economic sphere is now understood and recognized. The welfare of the part means the welfare of the whole, and the distress of the part brings distress to the whole. (Shoghi Effendi, *The Promised Day Is Come*, ¶300)

He [Bahá'u'lláh] as well as 'Abdu'l-Bahá after Him, has, unlike the Dispensations of the past, clearly and specifically laid down a set of Laws, established definite institutions, and provided for the essentials of a Divine Economy. (Shoghi Effendi, *The World Order of Bahá'u'lláh*, p. 19)

The economic teachings of the Cause, though well known in their main outline, have not as yet been sufficiently elaborated and systematized to allow anyone to make an exact and thorough application of them even on a restricted scale. (Shoghi Effendi, *Directives from the Guardian*, p. 19)

Only those who have already recognized the supreme station of Bahá'u'lláh, only those whose hearts have been touched by His love, and have become familiar with the potency of His spirit, can adequately appreciate the value of this Divine Economy—His inestimable gift to mankind. (Shoghi Effendi, *The World Order of Bahá'u'lláh*, p. 23)

The crisis that exists in the world is not confined to farmers. Its effects have reached every means of livelihood. (From a letter written on behalf of Shoghi Effendi, dated 2 March 1932, to an individual, in *Agriculture and Rural Life*)

Regarding your questions concerning the Bahá'í attitude on various economic problems, such as the problem of ownership, control and distribution of capital, and of other means of production, the problem of trusts and monopolies, and such economic experiments as social cooperatives; the Teachings of Bahá'u'lláh and 'Abdu'l-Bahá do not provide specific and detailed solutions to all such economic questions which mostly pertain to the domain of technical economics, and as such do not concern directly the Cause. True, there are certain guiding principles in Bahá'í Sacred Writings on the subject of economics, but these do by no means cover the whole field of theoretical and applied economics, and are mostly intended to guide further Bahá'í economic writers and technicians to evolve an economic system which would function in full conformity with the spirit and the exact provisions of the Cause on this and similar subjects. The International House of Justice will have, in consultation with economic experts, to assist in the formulation and evolution of the Bahá'í economic system of the future. One thing, however, is certain, that the Cause neither accepts the theories of the Capitalistic economics in full, nor can it agree with the Marxists and Communists in their repudiation of the principle of private ownership and of the vital sacred rights of the individual. (From a letter written on behalf of Shoghi Effendi, dated 10 June 1939, to an individual)

As regards your suggestion to write a book on Bahá'í economics; the Guardian has no objection to your writing such a work, but he feels that the task is a tremendously difficult one, specially in view of the fact that there are almost no specific teachings on technical economics as it is known and taught today. The Bahá'í Writings give us only a few principles which can guide future Bahá'í economists in their efforts to bring about the necessary readjustments in the economic and industrial system. (From a letter written on behalf of Shoghi Effendi, dated 30 June 1936, to an individual)

He does not think that we can yet go so far as to write commentaries and lengthy treatises on the relation of the Bahá'í teachings to Education, Economics, etc., as the world knows these subjects at present. We have our basic principles, but . . . (unreadable) We cannot say in detail what the "Bahá'í" system will be. It has yet to grow and mature. However, articles on these matters, where our general ideas are correlated to present knowledge and usage, and compared, would be good because not too much detail could be gone into. (From a letter written on behalf of Shoghi Effendi, dated 11 June 1948, in *Lights of Guidance*, Vol. 2, pp. 77–78)

Although Bahá'u'lláh does not set out in His Revelation a detailed economic system, a constant theme throughout the entire corpus of His teachings is the reorganization of human society. Consideration of this theme inevitably gives rise to questions of economics. Of course, the future order conceived by Bahá'u'lláh is far beyond anything that can be imagined by the present generation. Nevertheless, its eventual emergence will depend on strenuous effort by His followers to put His teachings into effect today. . . . (The Universal House of Justice, message dated 1 March 2017, to the Bahá'ís of the World)

In the field of social and economic development a tempo has been attained that impresses ever more deeply the effects of institutional and individual effort on both the internal development of the community and the community's collaboration with others. The Office of Social and Economic Development reports that during the second year of the Plan eight new Bahá'í-inspired development agencies were established, operating in such diverse fields as the advancement of women, health, agriculture , child education and youth empowerment. (The Universal House of Justice, Riḍván 2003, to the Bahá'ís of the World)

The economic theories of impersonal markets, promoting self-centered actions of individuals, have not helped humanity escape the extremes of poverty on the one hand and over-consumption on the other. New economic theories for our time must be animated by a motive beyond just profit. They must be rooted in the very human and relational dimension of all economic activity, which binds us as families, as communities and as citizens of one world. (Bahá'í International Community, "Eradicating Poverty: Moving Forward as One," the Bahá'í International Community's Statement on Poverty, 14 February 2008)

Access to development programs and their benefits must be ensured for all. (Bahá'í International Community, "Valuing Spirituality in Development: Initial Considerations Regarding the Creation of Spiritually Based Indicators for Development." A concept paper written for the World Faiths and Development Dialogue, Lambeth Palace, London, 18–19 February 1998)

Society must develop new economic models shaped by insights that arise from a sympathetic understanding of shared experience, from viewing human beings in relation one to another, and from a recognition of the central role that family and community play in social and spiritual well-being. Within institutions and organizations, priorities must be reassessed. Resources must be directed away from those agencies and programs that are damaging to the individual, societies and the environment, and directed toward those most germane to furthering a dynamic, just and thriving social order. Such economic systems will be strongly altruistic and cooperative in nature; they will provide meaningful employment and will help to eradicate poverty in the world. (Bahá'í International Community, "Valuing Spirituality in Development: Initial Considerations Regarding the Creation of Spiritually Based Indicators for Development." A concept paper written for the World Faiths and Development Dialogue, Lambeth Palace, London, 18–19 February 1998)

Development, for Bahá'ís, implies a dynamic coherence between the spiritual and material requirements of life on earth. The Bahá'í approach to development is organic and seeks to harmonize the seemingly paradoxical concepts of globalism and decentralization. Overall direction and guiding principles are established on the international—and often national—levels, helping to ensure a sense of global process and mission in all development activities. At the same time, actual programs and activities arise largely from individual or community initiative, are driven by community decision-making processes and are based on the principle of universal participation. They are, therefore, likely to address the needs, conditions and aspirations of the local/national society. Because of this approach, it is not possible to detail the projects and programs that communities will undertake in the coming years; however, the broad features of future development activities can be suggested. (Bahá'í International Community, "Conservation and Sustainable Development in the Bahá'í Faith." Paper presented by the Bahá'í International Community to the Summit on the Alliance between Religions and Conservation, 3 May 1995)

In the years immediately ahead, the Bahá'í world community will, no doubt, expand the scope and range of its conservation and sustainable development initiatives, while continuing along the lines already established including—education and training efforts focusing on conservation issues;—projects, both individual and community-based, aimed at the protection and restoration of the environment;—the use of the arts to inspire an active commitment to environmental protection and development; and—advocacy for sustainable development at local, national, and international levels. (Bahá'í International Community, "Conservation and Sustainable

Development in the Bahá'í Faith." Paper presented by the Bahá'í International Community to the Summit on the Alliance between Religions and Conservation, 3 May 1995)

BUILDING A SPIRITUAL FOUNDATION

The well-being of mankind, its peace and security, are unattainable unless and until its unity is firmly established. This unity can never be achieved so long as the counsels which the Pen of the Most High hath revealed are suffered to pass unheeded. (Bahá'u'lláh, *Gleanings from the Writings of Bahá'u'lláh,* no. 131.2)

Now is the time to cheer and refresh the down-cast through the invigorating breeze of love and fellowship, and the living waters of friendliness and charity. (Bahá'u'lláh, *Gleanings from the Writings of Bahá'u'lláh,* no. 5.1)

O Children of Dust! Tell the rich of the midnight sighing of the poor, lest heedlessness lead them into the path of destruction, and deprive them of the Tree of Wealth. To give and to be generous are attributes of Mine; well is it with him that adorneth himself with My virtues. (Bahá'u'lláh, The Hidden Words, Persian, no. 49)

O Son of Spirit! I created thee rich, why dost thou bring thyself down to poverty? Noble I made thee, wherewith dost thou abase thyself? Out of the essence of knowledge I gave thee being, why seekest thou enlightenment from anyone beside Me? Out of the clay of love I molded thee, how dost thou busy thyself with another? Turn thy sight unto thyself, that thou mayest find Me standing within thee, mighty, powerful and self-subsisting. (Bahá'u'lláh, The Hidden Words, Arabic, no. 13)

165

Say: Pride not yourselves on earthly riches ye possess. Reflect upon your end and upon the recompense for your works that hath been ordained in the Book of God, the Exalted, the Mighty. Blessed is the rich man whom earthly possessions have been powerless to hinder from turning unto God, the Lord of all names. Verily he is accounted among the most distinguished of men before God, the Gracious, the All-Knowing. (Bahá'u'lláh, *Ḥuqúqu'lláh—The Right of God: A Compilation of Extracts from the Writings of Bahá'u'lláh and 'Abdu'l-Bahá and from Letters Written by and on behalf of Shoghi Effendi and the Universal House of Justice,* 2009)

Be generous in prosperity, and thankful in adversity. Be worthy of the trust of thy neighbor, and look upon him with a bright and friendly face. Be a treasure to the poor, an admonisher to the rich, an answerer to the cry of the needy, a preserver of the sanctity of thy pledge. Be fair in thy judgment, and guarded in thy speech. Be unjust to no man, and show all meekness to all men. Be as a lamp unto them that walk in darkness, a joy to the sorrowful, a sea for the thirsty, a haven for the distressed, an upholder and defender of the victim of oppression. Let integrity and uprightness distinguish all thine acts. Be a home for the stranger, a balm to the suffering, a tower of strength for the fugitive. Be eyes to the blind, and a guiding light unto the feet of the erring. Be an ornament to the countenance of truth, a crown to the brow of fidelity, a pillar of the temple of righteousness, a breath of life to the body of mankind, an ensign of the hosts of justice, a luminary above the horizon of virtue, a dew to the soil of the human heart, an ark on the ocean of knowledge, a sun in the heaven of bounty, a gem on the diadem of wisdom, a shining light in the firmament of thy generation, a fruit upon the tree of humility. (Bahá'u'lláh, *Gleanings from the Writings of Bahá'u'lláh,* no. 130.1)

It is incumbent upon thee, and upon the followers of Him Who is the Eternal Truth, to summon all men to whatsoever shall sanctify them from all attachment to the things of the earth and purge them from its defilements, that the sweet smell of the raiment of the All-Glorious may be smelled from all them that love Him.

They who are possessed of riches, however, must have the utmost regard for the poor, for great is the honor destined by God for those poor who are steadfast in patience. By My life! There is no honor, except what God may please to bestow, that can compare to this honor. Great is the blessedness awaiting the poor that endure patiently and conceal their sufferings, and well is it with the rich who bestow their riches on the needy and prefer them before themselves.

Please God, the poor may exert themselves and strive to earn the means of livelihood. This is a duty which, in this most great Revelation, hath been prescribed unto every one, and is accounted in the sight of God as a goodly deed. Whoso observeth this duty, the help of the invisible One shall most certainly aid him. He can enrich, through His grace, whomsoever He pleaseth. He, verily, hath power over all things. (Bahá'u'lláh, *Gleanings from the Writings of Bahá'u'lláh*, no. 100.3–5)

Again, is there any deed in the world that would be nobler than service to the common good? Is there any greater blessing conceivable for a man, than that he should become the cause of the education, the development, the prosperity and honor of his fellow-creatures? No, by the Lord God! The highest righteousness of all is for blessed souls to take hold of the hands of the helpless and deliver them out of their ignorance and abasement and poverty, and with pure motives, and only for the sake of God, to arise and energetically devote themselves to the service of the masses, forgetting their own worldly advantage and working only to serve the general good. "They prefer them before themselves, though poverty be their own lot." The best of men are those who serve the people; the worst of men are those who harm the people. ('Abdu'l-Bahá, *The Secret of Divine Civilization*, ¶182)

Man reacheth perfection through good deeds, voluntarily performed, not through good deeds the doing of which was forced upon him. And sharing is a personally chosen righteous act: that is, the rich should extend assistance to the poor, they should expend their substance for the poor, but of their own free will, and not because the poor have gained this end by force. For the harvest of force is turmoil and the ruin of the social order. On the other hand voluntary sharing, the freely chosen expending of one's substance, leadeth to society's comfort and peace. It lighteth up the world; it bestoweth honor upon humankind. ('Abdu'l-Bahá, *Selections from the Writings of 'Abdu'l-Bahá*, no. 79.3)

I pray that you attain to such a degree of good character and behavior that the names of black and white shall vanish. All shall be called human, just as the name for a flight of doves is dove. They are not called black and white. ('Abdu'l-Bahá, *The Promulgation of Universal Peace*, p. 62)

When the love of God is established, everything else will be realized. This is the true foundation of all economics. Reflect upon it. Endeavor to become the cause of the attraction of souls rather than to enforce minds. ('Abdu'l-Bahá, *The Promulgation of Universal Peace*, p. 334)

"Economy is the foundation of human prosperity. . . . It is more kingly to be satisfied with a crust of stale bread than to enjoy a sumptuous dinner of many courses, the money for which comes out of the pockets of others. The mind of a contented person is always peaceful and his heart at rest. How happily such a man helps himself to his frugal meals! How joyfully he takes his walks, how peacefully he sleeps!" ('Abdu'l-Bahá, cited in J. E. Esslemont, *Bahá'u'lláh and the New Era*, p. 102)

Hearts must be so cemented together, love must become so dominant that the rich shall most willingly extend assistance to the poor and take steps to establish these economic adjustments permanently. If it is accomplished in this way, it will be most praiseworthy because then it will be for the sake of God and in the pathway of His service. For example, it will be as if the rich inhabitants of a city should say, "It is neither just nor lawful that we should possess great wealth while there is abject poverty in this community," and then willingly give their wealth to the poor, retaining only as much as will enable them to live comfortably. ('Abdu'l-Bahá, *The Promulgation of Universal Peace*, p. 334)

Then it is clear that the honour and exaltation of man cannot reside solely in material delights and earthly benefits. This material felicity is wholly secondary, while the exaltation of man resides primarily in such virtues and attainments as are the adornments of the human reality. These consist in divine blessings, heavenly bounties, heartfelt emotions, the love and knowledge of God, the education of the people, the perceptions of the mind, and the discoveries of science. They consist in justice and equity, truthfulness and benevolence, inner courage and innate humanity, safeguarding the rights of others and preserving the sanctity of covenants and agreements. They consist in rectitude of conduct under all circumstances, love of truth under all conditions, self-abnegation for the good of all people, kindness and compassion for all nations, obedience to the teachings of God, service to the heavenly Kingdom, guidance for all mankind, and education for all races and nations. This is the felicity of the human world! This is the exaltation of man in the contingent realm! This is eternal life and heavenly honour!

These gifts, however, do not manifest themselves in the reality of man save through a celestial and divine power and through the heavenly teachings, for they require a supernatural power. ('Abdu'l-Bahá, *Some Answered Questions*, no. 15.7–8)

Gracious God! How can one see one's fellow men hungry, destitute, and deprived, and yet live in peace and comfort in one's splendid mansion? How can one see others in the greatest need and yet take delight in one's fortune? That is why it has been decreed in the divine religions that the wealthy should offer up each year a portion of their wealth for the sustenance of the poor and the assistance of the needy. This is one of the foundations of the religion of God and is an injunction binding upon all. And since in this regard one is not outwardly compelled or obliged by the government, but rather aids the poor at the prompting of one's own heart and in a spirit of joy and radiance, such a deed is most commendable, approved, and pleasing. This is the meaning of the righteous deeds mentioned in the heavenly Books and Scriptures. ('Abdu'l-Bahá, *Some Answered Questions*, no. 78.12)

The Bahá'ís will bring about this improvement and betterment but not through sedition and appeal to physical force—not through warfare, but welfare. Hearts must be so cemented together, love must become so dominant that the rich shall most willingly extend assistance to the poor and take steps to establish these economic adjustments permanently. ('Abdu'l-Bahá, *The Promulgation of Universal Peace*, p. 334)

Shoghi Effendi was very glad to hear of your work among the ranchers. He sincerely hopes that they will advance in spirituality and become imbued with the spirit of Bahá'u'lláh. Country people should be much readier for the Message, for they are not so completely carried away by material civilization and its blinding influence. They ought to be more receptive and more pure in heart. (From a letter written on behalf of Shoghi Effendi, dated 13 May 1932, to an individual, in Universal House of Justice, Research Department, *Agriculture and Rural Life*, 1995)

Every choice [an individual] makes—as employee or employer, producer or consumer, borrower or lender, benefactor or beneficiary— leaves a trace, and the moral duty to lead a coherent life demands that one's economic decisions be in accordance with lofty ideals, that the purity of one's aims be matched by the purity of one's actions to fulfil those aims. . . . Not content with whatever values prevail in the existing order that surrounds them, the friends everywhere should consider the application of the teachings to their lives and, using the opportunities their circumstances offer them, make their own individual and collective contributions to economic justice and social progress wherever they reside. Such efforts will add to a growing storehouse of knowledge in this regard. (The Universal House of Justice, message dated 1 March 2017, to the Bahá'ís of the World)

In His Writings, Bahá'u'lláh states clearly the essential requisites for our spiritual growth, and these are reiterated and amplified by 'Abdu'l-Bahá in His talks and Tablets. They can be summarized briefly as prayer and meditation, the endeavor to conform one's behavior to the exalted standard set forth in the Bahá'í Teachings, participation in the life of the Bahá'í community, teaching the Faith and contributing to the Bahá'í Fund. Different individuals, according to their natures, will follow these paths in varying ways, but all are essential to spiritual growth. The House of Justice points out that there can be no rigid formula on how to attain the right balance in our approach to spirituality, and that the best course here, as in so many things, is to follow the example of 'Abdu'l-Bahá. (From a letter written on behalf of the Universal House of Justice, dated 22 April 1996, to an individual)

'Abdu'l-Bahá states that while "material civilization is one of the means for the progress of the world of mankind," until it is "combined with Divine civilization, the desired result, which is the felicity of mankind, will not be attained." He continues: Material civilization is like a lamp-glass. Divine civilization is the lamp itself and the glass without the light is dark. Material civilization is like the body. No matter how infinitely graceful, elegant and beautiful it may be, it is dead. Divine civilization is like the spirit, and the body gets its life from the spirit, otherwise it becomes a corpse. It has thus been made evident that the world of mankind is in need of the breaths of the Holy Spirit. Without the spirit the world of mankind is lifeless, and without this light the world of mankind is in utter darkness. (*Social Action*. A paper prepared by the Office of Social and Economic Development at the Bahá'í World Center, 26 November 2012)

Justice is the one power that can translate the dawning consciousness of humanity's oneness into a collective will through which the necessary structures of global community life can be confidently erected . . . it is the only means by which unity of thought and action can be achieved. (*The Prosperity of Humankind*. A statement prepared by the Bahá'í International Community Office of Public Information, Haifa, 1995)

Identifying the spiritual principles at the root of ecological challenges can also be key in formulating effective action. Principles—that humanity constitutes but a single people, for example, or that justice demands universal participation in the work of sustainable development—reflect the rich complexity of human nature. Just as importantly, they help foster the will and the aspiration needed to facilitate the implementation of pragmatic measures. Identifying the principles underlying given issues and formulating action in light of their imperatives is therefore a methodology that all can benefit from and contribute to—those in traditionally religious roles, but also leaders of government, the corporate sector, civil society, and others involved in the formulation of public policy. (Bahá'í International Community, "Shared Vision, Shared Volition: Choosing Our Global Future Together," a statement of the Bahá'í International Community to the United Nations Climate Change Conference in Paris, France, 23 November 2015)

Challenging ethical questions of resource distribution and responsibility for damages force governments to develop institutional mechanisms and implement policies that consider the prosperity and health of the global community and that of future generations. . . . At the educational level, curricula must seek to develop a sense of responsibility towards the natural environment as well as foster a spirit of inquiry and innovation so that the diversity of human experience can be brought to bear on the challenge of creating an environmentally sustainable development pathway. (Bahá'í International Community, "Eradicating Poverty: Moving Forward as One," the Bahá'í International Community's Statement on Poverty, 14 February 2008)

Moral reasoning, group decision-making and freedom from racism, for example, are all essential tools for poverty alleviation. Such capacities must shape individual thinking as well as institutional arrangements and policy-making. To be clear, the goal at hand is not only to remove the ills of poverty but to engage the masses of humanity in the construction of a just global order. (Bahá'í International Community, "Eradicating Poverty: Moving Forward as One," the Bahá'í International Community's Statement on Poverty, 14 February 2008)

One of the goals of poverty alleviation, then, centers on the individual: he must be helped to reclaim his dignity and sense of self-worth, must be encouraged to gain confidence to improve his condition and strive to realize his potential. Beyond the achievement of personal well-being, he must be nurtured to become a source of social good—of peace, happiness and advantage to those around him. It is at the level of service to others that our humanity achieves its highest expression. (Bahá'í International Community, "Eradicating Poverty: Moving Forward as One," the Bahá'í International Community's Statement on Poverty, 14 February 2008)

. . . such conditions as the marginalization of girls and women, poor governance, ethnic and religious antipathy, environmental degradation and unemployment constitute formidable obstacles to the progress and development of communities. These evidence a deeper crisis—one rooted in the values and attitudes that shape relationships at all levels of society. Viewed from this perspective, poverty can be described as the absence of those ethical, social and material resources needed to develop the moral, intellectual and social capacities of individuals, communities and institutions. Moral reasoning, group decision-making and freedom from racism, for example, are all essential tools for poverty alleviation. (Bahá'í International Community, "Eradicating Poverty: Moving Forward as One," the Bahá'í International Community's Statement on Poverty, 14 February 2008)

. . . there is increasing recognition that the world is in urgent need of a new "work ethic." Here again, nothing less than insights generated by the creative interaction of the scientific and religious systems of knowledge can produce so fundamental a reorientation of habits and attitudes. Unlike animals, which depend for their sustenance on whatever the environment readily affords, human beings are impelled to express the immense capacities latent within them through productive work designed to meet their own needs and those of others. In acting thus they become participants, at however modest a level, in the processes of the advancement of civilization. They fulfill purposes that unite them with others. To the extent that work is consciously undertaken in a spirit of service to humanity, Bahá'u'lláh says, it is a form of prayer, a means of worshiping God. Every individual has the capacity to see himself or herself in this light, and it is to this inalienable capacity of the self that development strategy must appeal, whatever the nature of the plans being pursued, whatever the rewards they promise. No narrower a perspective will ever call up from the people of the world the magnitude of effort and commitment that the economic tasks ahead will require. (*The Prosperity of Humankind*. A statement prepared by the Bahá'í International Community Office of Public Information, Haifa, 1995)

Qualities such as the capacity to sacrifice for the well-being of the whole, to trust and be trustworthy, to find contentment, to give freely and generously to others derive not from mere pragmatism or political expediency. Rather they arise from the deepest sources of human inspiration and motivation. In this, faith has shown itself to be key, whether in the efficacy of sustainability efforts or the capacity of the human race. (Bahá'í International Community, "Shared Vision, Shared Volition: Choosing Our Global Future Together," a statement of the Bahá'í International Community to the United Nations Climate Change Conference in Paris, France, 23 November 2015)

Human behavior and personal decision-making are therefore critical to the success of sustainability efforts, particularly in the sphere of values, ethics, and morals. Such qualities might seem diffuse or somewhat "soft," but changes in lifestyle will not be sustained if normative drivers of behaviors such as attitudes and beliefs do not shift as well. Consumption habits will not change if acquisition and the ongoing accumulation of luxury goods are seen as powerful symbols of success and importance. Building more sustainable patterns of life will therefore require continuing conversation about human nature and prerequisites for well-being. (Bahá'í International Community, "Shared Vision, Shared Volition: Choosing Our Global Future Together," a statement of the Bahá'í International Community to the United Nations Climate Change Conference in Paris, France, 23 November 2015)

"Nature in its essence is the embodiment of My Name, the Maker, the Creator. Its manifestations are diversified by varying causes, and in this diversity there are signs for men of discernment. Nature is God's Will and is its expression in and through the contingent world. It is a dispensation of Providence ordained by the Ordainer, the All-Wise. . . ." With those words, Bahá'u'lláh, Prophet-Founder of the Bahá'í Faith, outlines the essential relationship between man and the environment: that the grandeur and diversity of the natural world are purposeful reflections of the majesty and bounty of God.

For Bahá'ís, there follows an implicit understanding that nature is to be respected and protected, as a divine trust for which we are answerable. . . .

The major issues facing the environmental movement today hinge on this point. The problems of ocean pollution, the extinction of species, acid rain and deforestation—not to mention the ultimate scourge of nuclear war—respect no boundaries. All require a transnational approach. While all religious traditions point to the kind of cooperation and harmony that will indeed be necessary to curb these threats, the religious writings of the Bahá'í Faith also contain an explicit prescription for the kind of new world political order that offers the only long-term solution to such problems. "That which the Lord hath ordained as the sovereign remedy and mightiest instrument for the healing of the world is the union of all its people in one universal Cause," Bahá'u'lláh wrote. Built around the idea of the world commonwealth of nations, with an international parliament and executive to carry out its will, such a new political order must also, according to the Bahá'í teachings, be based on principles of economic justice, equality between the races, equal rights for women and men and universal education. All these points bear squarely on any attempt to protect the world's environment. The issue of economic justice is an example. In many regions of the world, the assault on rain forests and endangered species comes as the poor, legitimately seeking a fair share of the world's wealth, fell trees to create fields. They are unaware that, over the long term and as members of a world community which they know little about, they may be irretrievably damaging rather than improving their children's chances for a better life. Any attempt to protect nature, must, therefore, also address the fundamental inequities between the world's rich and poor. Likewise, the uplifting of women to full equality with men can help the environmental cause by bringing a new spirit of feminine values into decision-making about natural resources. The scriptures of the Bahá'í Faith note that: ". . . man has dominated over woman by reason of his more forceful and aggressive qualities both of body and mind. But the balance is already shifting; force is losing its dominance, and mental alertness, intuition and the spiritual qualities of love and service, in which woman is strong, are gaining ascendancy. Hence the new age will be an age less masculine and more permeated with feminine ideals . . . ." Education, especially an education that emphasizes Bahá'í principles of human interdependence, is another prerequisite to the building of a global conservation consciousness. The Faith's theology of unity and interdependence relates specifically to environmental issues. Again, to quote Bahá'í sacred writings: "By nature is meant those inherent properties and necessary relations derived from the realities of things. And these realities of things, though in the utmost diversity, are yet intimately connected one with the other . . . Liken the world of existence to the temple of man. All the organs of the human body assist one another, therefore life continues . . . Likewise among the parts of existence there is a wonderful connection and interchange of forces which is the cause of life of the world and the continuation of these countless phenomena." . . . Bahá'u'lláh, for example, clearly address the need to protect animals. "Look not upon the creatures of God except with the eye of kindliness and of mercy, for Our loving providence hath pervaded all created things, and Our grace encompassed the earth and the heavens." He Himself expressed a keen love and appreciation for nature, furthering the connection between the environment and the spiritual world in Bahá'í theology. "The country is the world of the soul, the city is the world of bodies," Bahá'u'lláh said. . . . For Bahá'ís the goal of existence is to carry forward an ever-advancing civilization. Such a civilization can only be built on an earth that can sustain itself. The Bahá'í commitment to the environment is fundamental to our Faith. (Bahá'í International Community, "The Bahá'í Statement on Nature," 1987)

STEWARDHSIP

Every man of discernment, while walking upon the earth, feeleth indeed abashed, inasmuch as he is fully aware that the thing which is the source of his prosperity, his wealth, his might, his exaltation, his advancement and power is, as ordained by God, the very earth which is trodden beneath the feet of all men. There can be no doubt that whoever is cognizant of this truth, is cleansed and sanctified from all pride, arrogance, and vainglory. (Bahá'u'lláh, *Epistle to the Son of the Wolf,* p. 44)

Were one to observe with an eye that discovereth the realities of all things, it would become clear that the greatest relationship that bindeth the world of being together lieth in the range of created things themselves, and that cooperation, mutual aid and reciprocity are essential characteristics in the unified body of the world of being, inasmuch all created things are closely related together and each is influenced by the other or deriveth benefit therefrom, either directly or indirectly. ('Abdu'l-Bahá, from a previously untranslated Tablet, in Bahá'í International Community, "Conservation and Sustainable Development in the Bahá'í Faith," 3 May 1995. This paper was presented by the Bahá'í International Community to the Summit on the Alliance Between Religions and Conservation)

This earth, these great mountains, the animals with their wonderful powers and instincts cannot go beyond natural limitations. All things are captives of nature except man. Man is the sovereign of nature;

he breaks nature's laws. . . . Man is gifted with a power whereby he penetrates and discovers the laws of nature, brings them forth from the world of invisibility into the plane of visibility. ('Abdu'l-Bahá, *The Promulgation of Universal Peace*, p. 361)

DESIRE TO EXPRESS TO HIS MAJESTY THE KING OR HIS MAJESTY'S REPRE-SENTATIVE AS WELL AS TO ASSEMBLED GUESTS MY HOPE WORK OF MEN OF TREES SO IMPORTANT FOR PROTECTION PHYSICAL WORLD AND HERITAGE FUTURE GENERATIONS MAY BE RICHLY BLESSED AND AT SAME TIME CON-STITUTE YET ANOTHER FORCE WORKING FOR PEACE AND BROTHERHOOD IN THIS SORELY TRIED DIVIDED WORLD. (Shoghi Effendi, cable dated 23 May 1951, to New Earth Luncheon, London)

We cannot segregate the human heart from the environment outside us and say that once one of these is reformed everything will be improved. Man is organic with the world. His inner life moulds the environment and is itself also deeply affected by it. The one acts upon the other and every abiding change in the life of man is the result of these mutual reactions. (From a letter written on behalf of Shoghi Effendi, dated 17 February 1933, to an individual)

DELIGHTED STEADY PROGRESS ACHIEVED MEN OF THE TREES WORLD OVER ESPECIALLY HOPES PLAN RECLAMATION DESERT AREAS AFRICA. (Cable on behalf of Shoghi Effendi, dated 22 May 1957, to World Forestry Charter Luncheon, London)

Creation reflects the names and attributes of God, and mankind has a profound responsibility to protect the natural environment and preserve its ecological balance. (The Universal House of Justice, *The Six Year Plan: Summary of Achievements*, p. 75)

. . . at a time when nations have difficulty reaching agreement on many important issues, the governments of nearly every country on earth have reached political consensus on a joint framework, in the Paris accord, to respond to climate change in a manner that is anticipated to evolve over time as experience accumulates. More than a century ago, 'Abdu'l-Bahá referred to "unity of thought in world undertakings, the consummation of which will erelong be witnessed." The recently adopted international agreement on climate change, irrespective of any shortcomings and limitations it may have, offers another noteworthy demonstration of that development anticipated by 'Abdu'l-Bahá. The agreement represents a starting point for constructive thought and action that can be refined or revised on the basis of experience and new findings over time. (From a letter written on behalf of the Universal House of Justice, dated 29 November 2017, to three individuals)

While as a fundamental principle Bahá'ís do not engage in partisan political affairs, this should not be interpreted in a manner that prevents the friends from full and active participation in the search for solutions to the pressing problems facing humanity. (From a letter written on behalf of the Universal House of Justice, dated 29 November 2017, to three individuals)

Shoghi Effendi links the preservation and reclamation of the earth's resources with both the "protection of the physical world and [the] heritage [of] future generations." He affirms that the work of such groups as the Men of the Trees and the World Forestry Charter is "essentially humanitarian," and he applauds their "noble objective" of reclaiming the "desert areas [of] Africa." (Research Department of the Universal House of Justice, "Conservation of the Earth's Resources," in *Compilation of Compilations*, Vol. 1, p. 83)

While the world of nature stands in need of development, man's approach to such development must be tempered by moderation, a commitment to protecting the "heritage [of] future generations," and an awareness of the sanctity of nature that pervades the Writings of the Bahá'í Faith. For example, Bahá'u'lláh states: "Blessed is the spot, and the house, and the place, and the city, and the heart, and the mountain, and the refuge, and the cave, and the valley, and the land, and the sea, and the island, and the meadow where mention of God hath been made, and His praise glorified." (Research Department of the Universal House of Justice, "Conservation of the Earth's Resources," in *Compilation of Compilations*, Vol. 1, p. 83)

In light of the interdependence and reciprocity of all parts of nature, the evolutionary perfection of all beings, and the importance of diversity "to the beauty, efficiency and perfection of the whole," it is clear to Bahá'ís that, in the ordering of human affairs, every effort should be made to preserve as much as possible the earth's biodiversity and natural order. (Bahá'í International Community, "Conservation and Sustainable Development in the Bahá'í Faith," paper presented by the Bahá'í International Community to the Summit on the Alliance Between Religions and Conservation, 3 May 1995)

Only a comprehensive vision of a global society, supported by universal values and principles, can inspire individuals to take responsibility for the long-term care and protection of the natural environment. Bahá'ís find such a world-embracing vision and system of values in the teachings of Bahá'u'lláh—teachings which herald an era of planetary justice, prosperity and unity. (Bahá'í International Community, "Conservation and Sustainable Development in the Bahá'í Faith," paper presented by the Bahá'í International Community to the Summit on the Alliance Between Religions and Conservation, 3 May 1995)

Bahá'í Scriptures describe nature as a reflection of the sacred. They teach that nature should be valued and respected, but not worshipped; rather, it should serve humanity's efforts to carry forward an ever-advancing civilization. However, in light of the interdependence of all parts of nature, and the importance of evolution and diversity "to the beauty, efficiency and perfection of the whole," every effort should be made to preserve as much as possible the earth's bio-diversity and natural order. . . . (Bahá'í International Community, "Valuing Spirituality in Development: Initial Considerations Regarding the Creation of Spiritually Based Indicators for Development," a concept paper written for the World Faiths and Development Dialogue, Lambeth Palace, London, 18–19 February 1998)

As trustees, or stewards, of the planet's vast resources and biological diversity, humanity must learn to make use of the earth's natural resources, both renewable and non-renewable, in a manner that ensures sustainability and equity into the distant reaches of time. This attitude of stewardship will require full consideration of the potential environmental consequences of all development activities. It will compel humanity to temper its actions with moderation and humility, realizing that the true value of nature cannot be expressed in economic terms. It will also require a deep understanding of the natural world and its role in humanity's collective development both material and spiritual. Therefore, sustainable environmental management must come to be seen not as a discretionary commitment mankind can weigh against other competing interests, but rather as a fundamental responsibility that must be shouldered a pre-requisite for spiritual development as well as the individual's physical survival. (Bahá'í International Community, "Valuing Spirituality in Development: Initial Considerations Regarding the Creation of Spiritually Based Indicators for Development," a concept paper written for the World Faiths and Development Dialogue, Lambeth Palace, London, 18–19 February 1998)

Exploring new patterns of interaction among the actors of society, such as individuals and institutions, will be central to the task of building more sustainable relationships with the natural world and among various segments of the global family. The work of addressing global climate change ultimately revolves around the aim of human lives well lived, which is a goal cherished by people and cultures the world over. In it can therefore be found a powerful point of unity to support the work ahead. We trust that the efforts of those at COP 21 will contribute to building a firm foundation on which the well-being and prosperity of humanity can be ever more effectively pursued for this and future generations. (Bahá'í International Community, "Shared Vision, Shared Volition: Choosing Our Global Future Together," a statement of the Bahá'í International Community to the United Nations Climate Change Conference in Paris, France, 23 November 2015)

Anthropogenic climate change is not inevitable; humanity chooses its relationships with the natural world. . . . The current global order has often approached the natural world as a reservoir of material resources to be exploited. The grave consequences of this paradigm have become all too apparent, and more balanced relationships among the peoples of the world and the planet are clearly needed. The question today is how new patterns of action and interaction can best be established, both individually and collectively, through personal choices, social systems, and governing institutions. (Bahá'í International Community, "Shared Vision, Shared Volition:

Choosing Our Global Future Together," a statement of the Bahá'í International Community to the United Nations Climate Change Conference in Paris, France, 23 November 2015)

For Bahá'ís, Bahá'u'lláh's promise that civilization will exist on this planet for a minimum of five thousand centuries makes it unconscionable to ignore the long-term impact of decisions made today. The world community must, therefore, learn to make use of the earth's natural resources, both renewable and non-renewable, in a manner that ensures sustainability into the distant reaches of time. This does not, however, mean that Bahá'ís advocate a "hands-off, back to the woods" policy. On the contrary, the world civilization that Bahá'ís believe will eventually emerge will be animated by a deep religious faith and will be one in which science and technology will serve humanity and help it to live in harmony with nature. (Bahá'í International Community, "Conservation and Sustainable Development in the Bahá'í Faith," a paper presented by the Bahá'í International Community to the Summit on the Alliance Between Religions and Conservation, 3 May 1995)

In the years immediately ahead, the Bahá'í world community will, no doubt, expand the scope and range of its conservation and sustainable development initiatives, while continuing along the lines already established including—education and training efforts focusing on conservation issues;—projects, both individual and community-based, aimed at the protection and restoration of the environment;—the use of the arts to inspire an active commitment to environmental protection and development; and—advocacy for sustainable development at local, national, and international levels. (Bahá'í International Community, "Conservation and Sustainable

Development in the Bahá'í Faith," a paper presented by the Bahá'í International Community to the Summit on the Alliance Between Religions and Conservation, 3 May 1995)

The Bahá'í world will work ceaselessly to develop in all its members—children, youth and adults—a deep respect for nature as a reflection of the majesty of the Divine, and a global consciousness based on the spiritual principles of unity in diversity, justice, love and service. (Bahá'í International Community, "Conservation and Sustainable Development in the Bahá'í Faith," a paper presented by the Bahá'í International Community to the Summit on the Alliance Between Religions and Conservation, 3 May 1995)

The most effective method to raise the consciousness of the worldwide Bahá'í community on the subject of climate change and to engage them in acts of service related to environmental sustainability is for the Institute to develop a course to explore the relationship of humans to the environment as articulated in the Bahá'í Sacred Writings. This course would not simply be aimed at increasing knowledge on the subject but, as mentioned above, would build the capacity of participants to engage in acts of service related to environmental sustainability. Similarly, the programs for children and junior youth would include material on climate change and the contribution that the younger generation can make to address the climate crisis. There are already examples of devotional gatherings in local communities that have chosen as their theme "care of the earth" or "the environment." Prayers, sacred writings and meditations during the devotional have elaborated this theme. Several children's classes offer acts of service to their communities. In some cases this action has been planting a community garden or cleaning up a stream or river. As this program is developed and used in communities throughout the world, such initiatives will be based on a better understanding of climate issues and the relevant Bahá'í perspective. Study, action and reflection on such action will result in a coherent framework for action on the subject of climate change. (Bahá'í International Community, "Bahá'í International Community's Plan of Action on Climate Change," 2009)

The changes required to reorient the world toward a sustainable future imply degrees of sacrifice, social integration, selfless action, and unity of purpose rarely achieved in human history. These qualities have reached their highest degree of development through the power of religion. Therefore, the world's religious communities have a major role to play in inspiring these qualities in their members, releasing latent capacities of the human spirit and empowering individuals to act on behalf of the planet, its peoples, and future generations. (Bahá'í International Community, "The Earth Charter/Rio De Janeiro Declaration and the Oneness of Humanity," UN, 1997)

Given their tremendous capacity to mobilize public opinion and their extensive reach in the most remote communities around the world, religious communities and their leaders bear an inescapable and weighty role in the climate change arena. By many measures, increasing numbers of religious communities are consistently lending their voice and resources to efforts to mitigate and adapt to the effects of climate change—they are educating their constituencies, providing a scriptural basis for ethical action and leading or participating in efforts at the national and international levels. (Bahá'í International Community, "Seizing the Opportunity: Redefining the challenge of climate change, Initial Considerations of the Bahá'í International Community," 1 December 2008)

The ongoing, vast extension of the gardens at the Bahá'í World Centre, including the erection of terraces from the foot to the summit of Mount Carmel, will increase the grandeur and majesty of this focal point of the Bahá'í World while providing an extended environment in which a deep respect for nature and a life-long commitment to its care and protection can be developed. Likewise, the grounds around Bahá'í properties, including Bahá'í Houses of Worship, will continue to be beautified to serve as an inspiration for all who visit them. (Bahá'í International Community, "Conservation and Sustainable Development in the Bahá'í Faith," a paper presented by the Bahá'í International Community to the Summit on the Alliance Between Religions and Conservation, 3 May 1995)

LAYING THE MATERIAL FOUNDATION

To give and be generous are attributes of Mine, well is it with him that adorneth himself with My virtues. (Bahá'u'lláh, The Hidden Words, Persian, no. 49)

Be generous in your days of plenty and be patient in the hour of loss. Adversity is followed by success and rejoicings follow woe. (Bahá'u'lláh, *Tablets of Bahá'u'lláh*, p. 138)

The beginning of magnanimity is when man expendeth his wealth on himself, on his family and on the poor among his brethren in his Faith. The essence of wealth is love for Me; whoso loveth Me is the possessor of all things, and he that loveth Me not is indeed of the poor and needy. This is that which the Finger of Glory and Splendor hath revealed. (Bahá'u'lláh, *Tablets of Bahá'u'lláh*, p. 156)

O Son of My Handmaid! Be not troubled in poverty nor confident in riches, for poverty is followed by riches, and riches are followed by poverty. Yet to be poor in all save God is a wondrous gift, belittle not the value thereof, for in the end it will make thee rich in God, and thus thou shalt know the meaning of the utterance, "In truth ye are the poor," and the holy words, "God is the all-possessing," shall even as the true morn break forth gloriously resplendent upon the horizon of the lover's heart, and abide secure on the throne of wealth. (Bahá'u'lláh, The Hidden Words, Persian, no. 51)

O Ye Rich Ones on Earth! The poor in your midst are My trust; guard ye My trust, and be not intent only on your own ease. (Bahá'u'lláh, The Hidden Words, Persian, no. 54)

O Ye that Pride Yourselves on Mortal Riches! Know ye in truth that wealth is a mighty barrier between the seeker and his desire, the lover and his beloved. The rich, but for a few, shall in no wise attain the court of His presence nor enter the city of content and resignation. Well is it then with him, who, being rich, is not hindered by his riches from the eternal kingdom, nor deprived by them of imperishable dominion. By the Most Great Name! The splendor of such a wealthy man shall illuminate the dwellers of heaven even as the sun enlightens the people of the earth! (Bahá'u'lláh, The Hidden Words, Persian, no. 53)

Please God, the poor may exert themselves and strive to earn the means of livelihood. This is a duty which, in this most great Revelation, hath been prescribed unto every one, and is accounted in the sight of God as a goodly deed. Whoso observeth this duty, the help of the invisible One shall most certainly aid him. He can enrich, through His grace, whomsoever He pleaseth. He, verily, hath power over all things. . . . (Bahá'u'lláh, *Gleanings from the Writings of Bahá'u'lláh*, no. 100.5)

Success or failure, gain or loss, must, therefore, depend upon man's own exertions. The more he striveth, the greater will be his progress. We fain would hope that the vernal showers of the bounty of God may cause the flowers of true understanding to spring from the soil of men's hearts, and may wash them from all earthly defilements. (Bahá'u'lláh, *Gleanings from the Writings of Bahá'u'lláh*, no. 34.8)

[I]f a person is incapable of earning a living, is stricken by dire poverty or becometh helpless, then it is incumbent on the wealthy or the Deputies to provide him with a monthly allowance for his subsistence. . . . By "Deputies" is meant the representatives of the people, that is to say the members of the House of Justice. ('Abdu'l-Bahá, in *The Kitáb-i-Aqdas*, Notes, no. 56)

And among the teachings of Bahá'u'lláh is voluntary sharing of one's property with others among mankind. This voluntary sharing is greater than equality, and consists in this, that man should not prefer himself to others, but rather should sacrifice his life and property for others. But this should not be introduced by coercion so that it becomes a law and man is compelled to follow it. Nay, rather, man should voluntarily and of his own choice sacrifice his property and life for others, and spend willingly for the poor. . . . ('Abdu'l-Bahá, *Selections from the Writings of 'Abdu'l-Bahá*, no. 227.19)

O Friends of God! Be ye assured that in place of these contributions, your agriculture, your industry, and your commerce will be blessed by manifold increases, with goodly gifts and bestowals. He who cometh with one goodly deed will receive a tenfold reward. There is no doubt that the living Lord will abundantly confirm those who expend their wealth in His path. ('Abdu'l-Bahá, from a Tablet translated from the Persian, in Universal House of Justice, Research Department, *Agriculture and Rural Life*, 1995)

It should not be imagined that the writer's earlier remarks constitute a denunciation of wealth or a commendation of poverty. Wealth is praiseworthy in the highest degree, if it is acquired by an individual's own efforts and the grace of God, in commerce, agriculture, art and industry, and if it be expended for philanthropic purposes. Above all, if a judicious and resourceful individual should initiate measures which would universally enrich the masses of the people, there could be no undertaking greater than this, and it would rank in the sight of God as the supreme achievement, for such a benefactor would supply the needs and insure the comfort and well-being of a great multitude. Wealth is most commendable, provided the entire population is wealthy. If, however, a few have inordinate riches while the rest are impoverished, and no fruit or benefit accrues from that wealth, then it is only a liability to its possessor. If, on the other hand, it is expended for the promotion of knowledge, the founding of elementary and other schools, the encouragement of art and industry, the training of orphans and the poor—in brief, if it is dedicated to the welfare of society—its possessor will stand out before God and man as the most excellent of all who live on earth and will be accounted as one of the people of paradise. ('Abdu'l-Bahá, *The Secret of Divine Civilization*, ¶46)

Every human being has the right to live; they have a right to rest, and to a certain amount of well-being. As a rich man is able to live in his palace surrounded by luxury and the greatest comfort, so should a poor man be able to have the necessaries of life. Nobody should die of hunger; everybody should have sufficient clothing; one man

should not live in excess while another has no possible means of existence. Let us try with all the strength we have to bring about happier
conditions, so that no single soul may be destitute. ('Abdu'l-Bahá,
Paris Talks, no. 40.23)

One of Bahá'u'lláh's teachings is the adjustment of means of livelihood in human society. Under this adjustment there can be no
extremes in human conditions as regards wealth and sustenance. For
the community needs financier, farmer, merchant and laborer just
as an army must be composed of commander, officers and privates.
All cannot be commanders; all cannot be officers or privates. Each
in his station in the social fabric must be competent—each in his
function according to ability but with justness of opportunity for
all. ('Abdu'l-Bahá, *The Promulgation of Universal Peace*, pp. 301–2)

The fundamental basis of the community is agriculture, tillage of the
soil. All must be producers. Each person in the community whose
need is equal to his individual producing capacity shall be exempt
from taxation. But if his income is greater than his needs, he must
pay a tax until an adjustment is effected. That is to say, a man's capacity for production and his needs will be equalized and reconciled
through taxation. If his production exceeds, he will pay a tax; if his
necessities exceed his production, he shall receive an amount sufficient to equalize or adjust. Therefore, taxation will be proportionate
to capacity and production, and there will be no poor in the community. ('Abdu'l-Bahá, *The Promulgation of Universal Peace*, p. 303)

A plan whereby all the individual members of society may enjoy the
utmost comfort and welfare. The degrees of society must be preserved. The farmer will continue to till the soil, the artist pursue
his art, the banker to finance the nations. An army has need of its

general, captain, and private soldiers. The degrees varying with the pursuits are essential. But in this Bahá'í plan there is no class hatred: Each is to be protected and each individual member of the body politic is to live in the greatest comfort and happiness. Work is to be provided for all and there will be no needy ones seen in the streets. ('Abdu'l-Bahá, in *Star of the West,* vol. 22, no. 1, p. 3)

One of the most important principles of the Teaching of Bahá'u'lláh is:

The right of every human being to the daily bread whereby they exist, or the equalization of the means of livelihood.

The arrangements of the circumstances of the people must be such that poverty shall disappear, that everyone, as far as possible, according to his rank and position, shall share in comfort and well-being.

We see amongst us men who are overburdened with riches on the one hand, and on the other those unfortunate ones who starve with nothing; those who possess several stately palaces, and those who have not where to lay their head. Some we find with numerous courses of costly and dainty food; whilst others can scarce find sufficient crusts to keep them alive. Whilst some are clothed in velvets, furs and fine linen, others have insufficient, poor and thin garments with which to protect them from the cold.

This condition of affairs is wrong, and must be remedied. Now the remedy must be carefully undertaken. It cannot be done by bringing to pass absolute equality between men. ('Abdu'l-Bahá, *Paris Talks,* no. 46.1–5)

It is therefore clearly established that the appropriation of excessive wealth by a few individuals, notwithstanding the needs of the masses, is unfair and unjust, and that, conversely, absolute equality would also disrupt the existence, welfare, comfort, peace, and orderly life of the human race. Such being the case, the best course is therefore to seek moderation, which is for the wealthy to recognize the advantages of moderation in the acquisition of profits and to show regard for the welfare of the poor and the needy, that is, to fix a daily wage for the workers and also to allot them a share of the total profits of the factory.

In brief, insofar as the mutual rights of the factory owners and the workers are concerned, laws must be enacted that would enable the former to make reasonable profits and the latter to be provided with their present necessities and their future needs, so that if they become incapacitated, grow old, or die and leave behind small children, they or their children will not be overcome by dire poverty but will receive a modest pension from the revenues of the factory itself. ('Abdu'l-Bahá, *Some Answered Questions*, no. 78.7–8)

A financier with colossal wealth should not exist whilst near him is a poor man in dire necessity. When we see poverty allowed to reach a condition of starvation it is a sure sign that somewhere we shall find tyranny. Men must bestir themselves in this matter, and no longer delay in altering conditions which bring the misery of grinding poverty to a very large number of the people. The rich must give of their abundance, they must soften their hearts and cultivate a compassionate intelligence, taking thought for those sad ones who are suffering from lack of the very necessities of life.

There must be special laws made, dealing with these extremes of riches and of want. The members of the Government should consider the laws of God when they are framing plans for the ruling of the people. The general rights of mankind must be guarded and preserved.

The government of the countries should conform to the Divine Law which gives equal justice to all. This is the only way in which the deplorable superfluity of great wealth and miserable, demoralizing, degrading poverty can be abolished. Not until this is done will the Law of God be obeyed. ('Abdu'l-Bahá, *Paris Talks,* no. 46.11–13)

Thus you can observe, on the one hand, a single person who has amassed a fortune, made an entire country his personal dominion, acquired immense wealth, and secured an unceasing flow of gains and profits, and, on the other, a hundred thousand helpless souls— weak, powerless, and wanting even a mouthful of bread . . . all the wealth, power, commerce, and industry are concentrated in the hands of a few individuals, while all others toil under the burden of endless hardships and difficulties, are bereft of advantages and benefits, and remain deprived of comfort and peace. One must therefore enact such laws and regulations as will moderate the excessive fortunes of the few and meet the basic needs of the myriad millions of the poor, that a degree of moderation may be achieved.

However, absolute equality is just as untenable, for complete equality in wealth, power, commerce, agriculture, and industry would result in chaos and disorder, disrupt livelihoods, provoke universal discontent, and undermine the orderly conduct of the affairs of the community. For unjustified equality is also fraught with peril. It is preferable, then, that some measure of moderation be achieved, and by moderation is meant the enactment of such laws and regulations as would prevent the unwarranted concentration of wealth in the hands of the few and satisfy the essential needs of the many. For instance, the factory owners reap a fortune every day, but the wage the poor workers are paid cannot even meet their daily needs: This is most unfair, and assuredly no just man can accept it. Therefore, laws and regulations should be enacted which would grant the workers both a daily wage and a share in a fourth or fifth of the profits of the factory in accordance with its means, or which would have the workers equitably share in some other way in the profits with the owners. For the capital and the management come from the latter and the toil and labour from the former. The workers could either be granted a wage that adequately meets their daily needs, as well as a right to a share in the revenues of the factory when they are injured, incapacitated, or unable to work, or else a wage could be set that allows the workers to both satisfy their daily needs and save a little for times of weakness and incapacity. . . .

The intervention of the government and the courts in the problems arising between owners and workers is fully warranted, since these are not such particular matters as are ordinary transactions between two individuals, which do not concern the public and in which the government should have no right to interfere. For problems between owners and workers, though they may appear to be a private matter, are detrimental to the common good, since the commercial, industrial, and agricultural affairs, and even the general business of the nation, are all intimately linked together: An impairment to one is a loss to all. And since the problems between owners and workers are detrimental to the common good, the government and the courts have therefore the right to intervene. ('Abdu'l-Bahá, *Some Answered Questions*, no. 78.4–5, 10)

The Bahá'ís will bring about this improvement and betterment but not through sedition and appeal to physical force—not through warfare, but welfare. Hearts must be so cemented together, love must become so dominant that the rich shall most willingly extend assistance to the poor and take steps to establish these economic adjustments permanently. ('Abdu'l-Bahá, *The Promulgation of Universal Peace*, p. 334)

With reference to Bahá'u'lláh's command concerning the engagement of the believers in some sort of profession: the Teachings are most emphatic on this matter, particularly the statement in the Aqdas to this effect which makes it quite clear that idle people who lack the desire to work can have no place in the new World Order. . . . Every individual, no matter how handicapped and limited he may be, is under the obligation of engaging in some work or profession, for work, especially when performed in the spirit of service, is according to Bahá'u'lláh a form of worship. It has not only a utilitarian purpose, but has a value in itself, because it draws us nearer to God, and enables us to better grasp His purpose for us in this world. It is obvious, therefore, that the inheritance of wealth cannot make anyone immune from daily work. (From a letter written on behalf of Shoghi Effendi, in *The Kitáb-i-Aqdas*, Notes, no. 56)

Whatever the progress of the machinery may be, man will always have to toil in order to earn his living. Effort is an inseparable part of man's life. It may take different forms with the changing conditions of the world, but it will be always present as a necessary element in our earthly existence. Life is after all a struggle. Progress is attained through struggle, and without such a struggle life ceases to have a meaning; it becomes even extinct. The progress of machinery has not made effort unnecessary. It has given it a new form, a new outlet. (From a letter written on behalf of Shoghi Effendi, dated 26 December 1935, in *Compilation of Compilations*, Vol. 3, p. 11)

He has noted with keen interest the plan you have conceived for the intensification of agricultural production with the view of meeting any possible food shortage in these times of war. While he is fully aware of the need for putting forth such a plan, and deeply appreciative as he feels of the noble motives that have prompted you to approach this problem, he nevertheless thinks that the time is not yet ripe for the believers, as a body, to undertake social and economic experiments of such character and scope. Neither the material resources at their disposal, nor their numerical strength are sufficient to give them any reasonable hope of embarking successfully upon a project of this kind. (From a letter written on behalf of Shoghi Effendi, dated 6 November 1940, to an individual believer, in Universal House of Justice, Research Department, *Extracts from the Bahá'í Writings on the Subject of Agriculture and Related Subjects*)

In Ecuador, as you no doubt know, the size of the Bahá'í community, scattered over inaccessible terrain in the high Andes, made it both necessary and possible some years ago to establish a Bahá'í radio station. "Radio Bahá'í," as it is known, broadcasts not only about the Faith, but has programs concerning health, agriculture, literacy and so on. It has now become so well established and highly regarded that it has been able to apply for and receive a Canadian Government grant through C.I.D.A to finance the development of certain social service activities. Thus it can be seen that once the Bahá'í community attains a certain stature it is able to work in fruitful collaboration with non-Bahá'í agencies in its social activities. (The Universal House of Justice, letter dated 3 January 1982, to an individual)

We need to start with an appropriate view of material wealth and its utilization. In the material world, to every end has been assigned a means for its accomplishment. Thus vigilance must be exercised in distinguishing "means" from "ends"; otherwise, what is intended as a mere instrument could easily become the very goal of an individual's life. The acquisition of wealth is a case in point; it is acceptable and praiseworthy to the extent that it serves as a means for achieving higher ends—for meeting one's basic necessities, for fostering the progress of one's family, for promoting the welfare of society, and for contributing to the establishment of a world civilization. But to make the accumulation of wealth the central purpose of one's life is unworthy of any human being. (The Universal House of Justice, message dated 2 April 2010, to Bahá'ís in the Cradle of the Faith)

That the development process is inherently complex is undeniable. It can involve activity in areas such as agriculture and animal husbandry, manufacturing and marketing, the management of funds and natural resources, health and sanitation, education and socialization, communication and community organization. The knowledge that must be brought to bear on the development concerns of the communities of the world, then, does not fit into a single area or discipline. Interdisciplinary and multisectoral action is clearly called for. Yet the capacity to pursue such coordinated action will only appear in the Bahá'í community over the course of decades, as will the capacity to address development issues at increasingly higher levels of complexity and effectiveness. (*Social Action.* A paper prepared by the Office of Social and Economic Development at the Bahá'í World Center, 26 November 2012)

The legitimacy of wealth depends, 'Abdu'l-Bahá has indicated, on how it is acquired and on how it is expended. In this connection, He has stated that "wealth is praiseworthy in the highest degree, if it is acquired by an individual's own efforts and the grace of God, in commerce, agriculture, crafts and industry," if the measures adopted by the individual in generating wealth serve to "enrich the generality of the people," and if the wealth thus obtained is expended for "philanthropic purposes" and "the promotion of knowledge," for the establishment of schools and industry and the advancement of education, and in general for the welfare of society. (The Universal House of Justice, message dated 2 April 2010, to the Believers in the Cradle of the Faith)

Bahá'í projects of social and economic development have greatly multiplied and brought much credit to the community in the examples of the power of group initiative and voluntary consultative action that have been set in numerous places. Activities in this respect involved more than one thousand projects in the areas of education, agriculture, health, literacy, the environment and improvement of the status of women. In a number of instances the projects benefited from collaboration with or assistance from governments and international nongovernmental organizations, as, for example, the projects for the improvement of the status of women undertaken by five National Spiritual Assemblies with the financial assistance of the United Nations Development Fund for Women (UNIFEM), and those projects in other fields receiving assistance from the Canadian, Indian, German and Norwegian governments. Some projects have been so distinguished in their achievements as to be given public notice through the citations and awards of governments and international nongovernmental agencies. (The Universal House of Justice, Riḍván 1992, to the Bahá'ís of the World)

All this has kept our beloved Faith under international observation, an interest increased not only by the circulation of the Peace Statement but also by the rapidly expanding activities in the field of economic and social development, ranging from the inauguration and operation of radio stations—of which there are seven now broadcasting—to schools, literacy programs, agricultural assistance and a host of small but valuable undertakings at village level in many parts of the world. (The Universal House of Justice, Riḍván 1987, to the Bahá'ís of the World)

HUQÚQU'LLÁH (THE RIGHT OF GOD)

Say: O people, the first duty is to recognize the one true God—magnified be His glory—the second is to show forth constancy in His Cause and, after these, one's duty is to purify one's riches and earthly possessions according to that which is prescribed by God. Therefore it beseemeth thee to meet thine obligation to the Right of God first, then to direct thy steps toward His blessed House. This hath been brought to thine attention as a sign of favor. (Bahá'u'lláh, in *Ḥuqúqu'lláh—The Right of God: A Compilation of Extracts from the Writings of Bahá'u'lláh and 'Abdu'l-Bahá and from Letters Written by and on Behalf of Shoghi Effendi and the Universal House of Justice*, 2009)

This is the Book of Generosity which hath been revealed by the King of Eternity. Whoso adorneth himself with this virtue hath distinguished himself and will be blessed by the All-Merciful from His exalted Kingdom of Glory. However, despite his high rank and prominent position, were he to pass beyond the limits, he would be regarded as among the prodigal by the All-Knowing, the All-Wise. Cling ye unto moderation. This is the commandment that He Who is the All-Possessing, the Most High hath enjoined upon you in His Generous Book. O ye that are the exponents of generosity and the manifestations thereof! Be generous unto them whom ye find in manifest poverty. O ye that are possessed of riches! Take heed lest outward appearance deter you from benevolent deeds in the path of God, the Lord of all mankind.

Say: I swear by God! No one is despised in the sight of the Almighty for being poor. Rather is he exalted, if he is found to be of them who are patient. Blessed are the poor that are steadfast in patience, and woe betide the rich that hold back Ḥuqúqu'lláh and fail to observe that which is enjoined upon them in His Preserved Tablet.

Say: Pride not yourselves on earthly riches ye possess. Reflect upon your end and upon the recompense for your works that hath been ordained in the Book of God, the Exalted, the Mighty. Blessed is the rich man whom earthly possessions have been powerless to hinder from turning unto God, the Lord of all names. Verily he is accounted among the most distinguished of men before God, the Gracious, the All-Knowing.

Say: The appointed Day is come. This is the Springtime of benevolent deeds, were ye of them that comprehend. Strive ye with all your might, O people, that ye may bring forth that which will truly profit you in the worlds of your Lord, the All-Glorious, the All-Praised.

Say: Hold ye fast unto praiseworthy characteristics and goodly deeds and be not of them that tarry. It behooveth everyone to cleave tenaciously unto that which is conducive to the exaltation of the Cause of God, your Lord, the Mighty, the Powerful.

Say: Behold ye not the world, its changes and chances, and its varying colours? Wherefore are ye satisfied with it and with all the things therein? Open your eyes and be of them that are endued with insight. The day is fast approaching when all these things will have vanished as fast as the lightning, nay even faster. Unto this beareth witness the Lord of the Kingdom in this wondrous Tablet.

Wert thou to be enraptured by the uplifting ecstasy of the verses of God, thou wouldst yield thanks unto thy Lord and say: "Praise be unto Thee, O Desire of the hearts of them that hasten to meet Thee!" Rejoice then with exceeding gladness, inasmuch as the Pen of Glory hath turned unto thee and hath revealed in thy honour that which the tongues of creation and the tongues of transcendence are powerless to describe. (Bahá'u'lláh, in *Ḥuqúqu'lláh—The Right of God: A Compilation of Extracts from the Writings of Bahá'u'lláh and 'Abdu'l-Bahá and from Letters Written by and on Behalf of Shoghi Effendi and the Universal House of Justice*, 2009)

It is clear and evident that the payment of the Right of God is conducive to prosperity, to blessing, and to honor and divine protection. Well is it with them that comprehend and recognize this truth and woe betide them that believe not. And this is on condition that the individual should observe the injunctions prescribed in the Book with the utmost radiance, gladness and willing acquiescence. It behooveth you to counsel the friends to do that which is right and praiseworthy. Whoso hearkeneth to this call, it is to his own behoof, and whoso faileth bringeth loss upon himself. Verily our Lord of Mercy is the All-Sufficing, the All-Praised. (Bahá'u'lláh, in *Ḥuqúqu'lláh—The Right of God: A Compilation of Extracts from the Writings of Bahá'u'lláh and 'Abdu'l-Bahá and from Letters Written by and on Behalf of Shoghi Effendi and the Universal House of Justice*, 2009)

All the world hath belonged and will always belong to God. If one spontaneously offereth Ḥuqúq with the utmost joy and radiance it will be acceptable, and not otherwise. The benefit of such deeds reverteth unto the individuals themselves. (Bahá'u'lláh, in *Ḥuqúqu'lláh—The Right of God: A Compilation of Extracts from the Writings of Bahá'u'lláh and 'Abdu'l-Bahá and from Letters Written by and on Behalf of Shoghi Effendi and the Universal House of Justice*, 2009)

Should anyone acquire one hundred mi<u>th</u>qáls of gold, nineteen mi<u>th</u>qáls thereof are God's and to be rendered unto Him, the Fash-

203

ioner of earth and heaven. Take heed, O people, lest ye deprive your-selves of so great a bounty. This We have commanded you, though We are well able to dispense with you and with all who are in the heavens and on earth; in it there are benefits and wisdoms beyond the ken of anyone but God, the Omniscient, the All-Informed. Say: By this means He hath desired to purify what ye possess and to en-able you to draw nigh unto such stations as none can comprehend save those whom God hath willed. He, in truth, is the Beneficent, the Gracious, the Bountiful. (Bahá'u'lláh, The Kitáb-i-Aqdas, ¶97)

Time and again have We written and commanded that no one should solicit such payment. The offering of every person that vol-untarily tendereth the Ḥuqúqu'lláh with the utmost joy and pleasure may be accepted, otherwise acceptance was not and is not permissi-ble. (Bahá'u'lláh, in *Ḥuqúqu'lláh—The Right of God: A Compilation of Extracts from the Writings of Bahá'u'lláh and 'Abdu'l-Bahá and from Letters Written by and on Behalf of Shoghi Effendi and the Universal House of Justice*, 2009)

The payment of the Right of God is conditional upon one's fi-nancial ability. If a person is unable to meet his obligation, God will verily excuse him. He is the All-Forgiving, the All-Generous. (Bahá'u'lláh, in *Ḥuqúqu'lláh—The Right of God: A Compilation of Extracts from the Writings of Bahá'u'lláh and 'Abdu'l-Bahá and from Letters Written by and on Behalf of Shoghi Effendi and the Universal House of Justice*, 2009)

The Primal Point hath directed that Ḥuqúqu'lláh must be paid on the value of whatsoever one possesseth; yet, in this Most Mighty Dispensation, We have exempted the household furnishings, that is such furnishings as are needed, and the residence itself. (Bahá'u'lláh, in *The Kitáb-i-Aqdas,* "Questions and Answers," p. 109)

It hath been decreed by God that a property which is not lucrative, that is, yieldeth no profit, is not subject to the payment of Ḥuqúq. Verily He is the Ordainer, the Bountiful. (Bahá'u'lláh, in *Ḥuqúqu'lláh—The Right of God: A Compilation of Extracts from the Writings of Bahá'u'lláh and 'Abdu'l-Bahá and from Letters Written by and on Behalf of Shoghi Effendi and the Universal House of Justice,* 2009)

Thou hast written that they have pledged themselves to observe maximum austerity in their lives with a view to forwarding the remainder of their income to His exalted presence. This matter was mentioned at His holy court. He said: Let them act with moderation and not impose hardship upon themselves. We would like them both to enjoy a life that is well-pleasing. (Bahá'u'lláh, in *Ḥuqúqu'lláh—The Right of God: A Compilation of Extracts from the Writings of Bahá'u'lláh and 'Abdu'l-Bahá and from Letters Written by and on Behalf of Shoghi Effendi and the Universal House of Justice,* 2009)

Know thou, moreover, that those who faithfully serve the All-Merciful will be enriched by Him out of His heavenly treasury, and that the Ḥuqúq offering is but a test applied by Him unto His servants and maidservants. Thus every true and sincere believer will offer Ḥuqúq to be expended for the relief of the poor, the disabled, the needy, and the orphans, and for other vital needs of the Cause of God, even as Christ did establish a Fund for benevolent purposes. ('Abdu'l-Bahá, in *Ḥuqúqu'lláh—The Right of God: A Compilation of*

Extracts from the Writings of Bahá'u'lláh and 'Abdu'l-Bahá and from Letters Written by and on Behalf of Shoghi Effendi and the Universal House of Justice, 2009)

Ḥuqúq is not payable on agricultural tools and equipment, and on animals used in ploughing the land to the extent that these are necessary. ('Abdu'l-Bahá, in *Ḥuqúqu'lláh—The Right of God: A Compilation of Extracts from the Writings of Bahá'u'lláh and 'Abdu'l-Bahá and from Letters Written by and on Behalf of Shoghi Effendi and the Universal House of Justice, 2009)*

Everything that a believer possesses, with the exception of certain specific items, is subject once and only once to the payment of Ḥuqúqu'lláh.

Exempt from assessment to Ḥuqúqu'lláh are:

1. The residence and its needful furnishings (11).

2. The needful business and agricultural equipment which produce income for one's subsistence (12, 67, 68). (The Universal House of Justice, message dated 26 November 2000, to all National Spiritual Assemblies)

It is clear from the Writings that a person is exempt from paying Ḥuqúqu'lláh on his residence and such household and professional equipment as are needful. It is left to the discretion of the individual to decide which items are necessary and which are not. It is obvious that the friends should not spend lavishly on residences and furnishings and rationalize on these expenditures in their desire to avoid payment of Ḥuqúqu'lláh. No specific text has been found exempting capital used to earn income. The Universal House of Justice leaves such matters to the consciences of individual believers. (The Universal House of Justice, letter dated 9 April 1980, in *Ḥuqúqu'lláh—The Right of God: A Compilation of Extracts from the Writings of Bahá'u'lláh and 'Abdu'l-Bahá and from Letters Written by and on Behalf of Shoghi Effendi and the Universal House of Justice*, 2009)

The institution of Ḥuqúqu'lláh will, during the course of this Dispensation, contribute to the spiritualization of humanity through the promotion of a new attitude to the acquisition and use of material resources. It will provide the material resources necessary for great collective enterprises designed to improve all aspects of life, and will be a powerful element in the growth of a world civilization. (The Universal House of Justice, message dated 12 January 2003, to the Deputies and Representatives of the institution of Ḥuqúqu'lláh)

Payment of Ḥuqúqu'lláh is a spiritual obligation binding on the people of Bahá. The injunction is laid down in the Most Holy Book, and clear and conclusive explanations are embodied in various Tablets. Every devoted believer who is able to meet the specified conditions, must pay the Ḥuqúqu'lláh, without any exception. (From a letter written on Behalf of the Universal House of Justice, dated 25 October 1970, to the National Spiritual Assembly of Iran in *Ḥuqúqu'lláh—The Right of God: A Compilation of Extracts from the Writings of Bahá'u'lláh and 'Abdu'l-Bahá and from Letters Written by and on Behalf of Shoghi Effendi and the Universal House of Justice*, 2009)

VILLAGE STOREHOUSE

In brief, from among the wise men in every village a board should be set up and the affairs of that village should be under the control of that board. Likewise a general storehouse should be founded with the appointment of a secretary. At the time of the harvest, under the direction of that board, a certain percentage of the entire harvest should be appropriated for the storehouse.

The storehouse has seven revenues: Tithes, taxes on animals, property without an heir, all lost objects found whose owners cannot be traced, one third of all treasure-trove, one third of the produce of all mines, and voluntary contributions.

This storehouse also has seven expenditures:

1. General running expenses of the storehouse, such as the salary of the secretary and the administration of public health.

2. Tithes to the government.

3. Taxes on animals to the government.

4. Costs of running an orphanage.

5. Costs of running a home for the incapacitated.

6. Costs of running a school.

7. Payment of subsidies to provide needed support of the poor.

The first revenue is the tithe. It should be collected as follows: If, for instance, the income of a person is five hundred dollars and his necessary expenses are the same, no tithes will be collected from him. If another's expenses are five hundred dollars while his income is one thousand dollars, one tenth will be taken from him, for he hath more than his needs; if he giveth one tenth of the surplus, his livelihood will not be adversely affected. If another's expenses are one thousand dollars, and his income is five thousand dollars, as he hath four thousand dollars surplus he will be required to give one and a half tenths. If another person hath necessary expenses of one thousand dollars, but his income is ten thousand dollars, from him two tenths will be required for his surplus represents a large sum. But if the necessary expenses of another person are four or five thousand dollars, and his income one hundred thousand, one fourth will be required from him. On the other hand, should a person's income be two hundred, but his needs absolutely essential for his livelihood be five hundred dollars, and provided he hath not been remiss in his work or his farm hath not been blessed with a harvest, such a one must receive help from the general storehouse so that he may not remain in need and may live in comfort.

A certain amount must be put aside from the general storehouse for the orphans of the village and a certain sum for the incapacitated. A certain amount must be provided from this storehouse for those who are needy and incapable of earning a livelihood, and a certain amount for the village's system of education. And, a certain amount must be set aside for the administration of public health. If anything is left in the storehouse, that must be transferred to the general treasury of the nation for national expenditures. ('Abdu'l-Bahá, *Pearls of Bounty*, no. 2.21.5)

As to the economic question, it hath been stated briefly and the basis of it hath been set forth, while its details are to be fixed by the Universal House of Justice. The board of the house of finance storehouse will direct in every village the revenues of the house, such as tithes, tax on animals, etc. In every village a storehouse and an officer in charge are to be provided, while the notables of the village gather and form a board and to this board and officer the direction of the affairs of the village are entrusted. They take charge of all questions pertaining to the village, and the revenues of the storehouse such as tithes, tax on animals and other revenues are gathered in it and are given out for necessary expenditures.

As to the doubling of tithes in accordance with the size of revenues and of crops: it is not possible to double as a fixed proportion the amount of tithes to be paid when the revenues are doubled. For instance, a man whose revenues amount to 1,000 dollars and whose expenses are 500 dollars, should pay one tenth of his revenues, i.e.,

100 dollars. When his revenues reach 2,000 dollars and his expenses remain 500 dollars, he cannot pay two tenths of his revenues, i.e. 400 dollars, for it would be difficult. At most he can pay 1.5 tenths, which is 300 dollars. If his revenues rise to 4,000 dollars, he can give 1.75 tenths of his revenues, i.e. 700 dollars, and if his revenues are 8,000 dollars, he can pay two tenths, i.e. 1,600 dollars, and if they still rise to 16,000 dollars, he can pay one fourth (2.5 tenths), i.e. 4,000 dollars. If they still rise to 32,000 dollars and the tithes to be taken from him were to be fixed at a definite ratio (i.e. doubled every time), they would constitute a huge amount which he would not be able to pay, as the preparation of the harvest entails many expenditures. Therefore, for a revenue of 16,000 dollars, one fourth is taken from him (two and a half tenths). In short the division and the fixing of everyone's share are to be arranged in accordance with the time and place by the House of Justice.

What hath been stated is only an example and this doth not mean that it should be enforced exactly in this manner. The principle is that as a man's wealth increaseth, his financial obligations should proportionately increase, so that vast riches may not be accumulated in one place. In this manner justice may be exercised between the rich and the poor. Thus there will not be, on one hand, a man owning a thousand million and, on the other, a poor man in need of his necessary subsistence. As to the revenues of the storehouse, the House of Justice must strive by every means possible to increase that amount, i.e. by every just means. Likewise with the expenditures; if anything is deemed necessary for the village such as the providing of hygienic measures, the House of Justice must also make all the necessary provisions. In short, if it is done in this manner in the village, the orphans, the disabled and the poor will secure the means of subsistence; education will be fostered, and the adoption of hygienic measures will become universal.

These are only the preliminary principles; the House of Justice will arrange and widen them in accordance with time and place. ('Abdu'l-Bahá, Tablet dated 25 July 1919, to an individual believer, in Universal House of Justice, Research Department, *Extracts from the Bahá'í Writings on the Subject of Agriculture and Related Subjects*, no. 9.3)

One of Bahá'u'lláh's teachings is the adjustment of means of livelihood in human society. Under this adjustment there can be no extremes in human conditions as regards wealth and sustenance. For the community needs financier, farmer, merchant and laborer just as an army must be composed of commander, officers and privates. All cannot be commanders; all cannot be officers or privates. Each in his station in the social fabric must be competent—each in his function according to ability but with justness of opportunity for all. . . . Difference of capacity in human individuals is fundamental. It is impossible for all to be alike, all to be equal, all to be wise. Bahá'u'lláh has revealed principles and laws which will accomplish the adjustment of varying human capacities. He has said that whatsoever is possible of accomplishment in human government will be effected through these principles. When the laws He has instituted are carried out, there will be no millionaires possible in the community and likewise no extremely poor. This will be effected and regulated by adjusting the different degrees of human capacity. The fundamental basis of the community is agriculture, tillage of the soil. All must be producers. Each person in the community whose need is equal to his individual producing capacity shall be exempt from taxation. But if his income is greater than his needs, he must pay a tax until an adjustment is effected. That is to say, a man's capacity for production and his needs will be equalized and reconciled through taxation. If his production exceeds, he will pay a tax; if his necessities exceed his production, he shall receive an amount sufficient to equalize or adjust. Therefore, taxation will be proportionate to capacity and production, and there will be no poor in the community. ('Abdu'l-Bahá, *The Promulgation of Universal Peace*, p. 475)

His Holiness Bahá'u'lláh has given instructions regarding every one of the questions confronting humanity. He has given teachings and instructions with regard to every one of the problems with which man struggles. Among them are (the teachings) concerning the question of economics that all the members of the body politic may enjoy through the working out of this solution the greatest happiness, welfare and comfort without any harm or injury attacking the general order of things. Thereby no difference or dissension will occur. No sedition or contention will take place. The solution is this:

First and foremost is the principle that to all the members of the body politic shall be given the greatest achievements of the world of humanity. Each one shall have the utmost welfare and well-being. To solve this problem we must begin with the farmer; there will we lay a foundation for system and order because the peasant class and the agricultural class exceed other classes in the importance of their service. In every village there must be established a general storehouse which will have a number of revenues.

The first revenue will be that of the tenth or tithes.

The second revenue [will be derived] from the animals.

The third revenue, from the minerals; that is to say, every mine prospected or discovered, a third thereof will go to this vast storehouse.

The fourth is this: whosoever dies without leaving any heirs, all his heritage will go to the general storehouse.

Fifth, if any treasures shall be found on the land, they should be devoted to this storehouse.

All these revenues will be assembled in this storehouse.

As to the first, the tenths or tithes: We will consider a farmer, one of the peasants. We will look into his income. We will find out for instance, what is his annual revenue and also what are his expenditures. Now, if his income be equal to his expenditures, from such a farmer nothing whatever will be taken. That is, he will not be subjected to taxation of any sort, needing as he does all his income. Another farmer may have expenses running up to one thousand dollars, we will say, and his income is two thousand dollars. From such an one a tenth will be required, because he has a surplus. But if his income be ten thousand dollars and his expenses one thousand dollars or his income twenty thousand dollars, he will have to pay as taxes, one fourth. If his income be one hundred thousand dollars, and his expenses five thousand, one third will he have to pay because he has still a surplus since his expenses are five thousand and his income one hundred thousand. If he pays, say, thirty-five thousand dollars, in addition to the expenditure of five thousand he still has sixty thousand left. But if his expenses be ten thousand and his income two hundred thousand, then he must give an even half because ninety thousand will be in that case the sum remaining. Such a scale as this will determine allotment of taxes. All the income from such revenues will go to this general storehouse.

Then there must be considered such emergencies as follows: A certain farmer whose expenses run up to ten thousand dollars and whose income is only five thousand will receive necessary expenses from the storehouse. Five thousand dollars will be allotted to him so he will not be in need.

Then the orphans will be looked after, all of whose expenses will be taken care of. The cripples in the village—all their expenses will be looked after. The poor in the village—their necessary expenses will be defrayed. And other members who for valid reasons are incapacitated—the blind, the old, the deaf—their comfort must be looked after. In the village no one will remain in need or in want. All will live in the utmost comfort and welfare. Yet no schism will assail the general order of the body politic.

Hence, the expenses or expenditures of the general storehouse are now made clear and its activities made manifest. The income of this general storehouse has been shown. Certain trustees will be elected by the people in a given village to look after these transactions. The farmers will be taken care of, and, if after all these expenses are defrayed, any surplus is found in the storehouse, it must be transferred to the national treasury.

This system is all thus ordered so that in the village the very poor will be comfortable, the orphans will live happily and well; in a word, no one will be left destitute. All the individual members of the body politic will thus live comfortably and well.

For larger cities, naturally, there will be a system on a larger scale. Were I to go into that solution the details thereof would be very lengthy.

The result of this [system] will be that each individual member of the body politic will live most comfortably and happily under obligation to no one. Nevertheless, there will be preservation of degree because in the world of humanity there must needs be degrees. The body politic may well be likened to an army. In this army there must be a general, there must be a sergeant, there must be a marshal, there must be the infantry; but all must enjoy the greatest comfort and welfare. ('Abdu'l-Bahá, *The Promulgation of Universal Peace*, pp. 437–38)

He was much interested in your ideas over the solution of the economic problem in the West—a question that must have meant a good deal of thought to many enlightened people—and he is delighted to see in your thoughts much that runs along the same gener-

214

al lines as the principles laid out by the Movement. Of course conditions in the East differ; where the countries are rarely industrial and mostly agricultural, we should have to apply different laws from the West, and that is why the principles of the Movement strike at the root which is common to them both. 'Abdu'l-Bahá has developed in various of His talks, which you will find in different compilations, the principles upon which the Bahá'í economic system would be based. A system that prevents, among others, the gradual control of wealth in the hands of a few and the resulting state of both extremes, wealth and poverty. (From a letter written on behalf of Shoghi Effendi, dated 28 October 1927, to an individual, in Universal House of Justice, Research Department, *Extracts from the Bahá'í Writings on the Subject of Agriculture and Related Subjects*)

Rural development is facilitated if the people of the villages are open to new ideas and receptive to innovation; under such conditions, they are likely to adopt more efficient agricultural techniques, to encourage their children to acquire education, and to practice good hygiene. Yet, so often, village people are apprehensive about the technological and social changes invading their settled way of life, are fearful of the future, and are uncertain whether there will be a place for them in the world of tomorrow. There is a pressing need for re-affirmation of the intrinsic worth of every individual human being, and for an over-riding recognition of the oneness of mankind. The values we call for are spiritual values, which will penetrate to the core of being and will create a sense of personal self-worth and security, freeing the individual to respond positively to innovative change. (Bahá'í International Community, "Spiritual and Social Values for Rural Development." Paper presented to the Twentieth Conference of the South Pacific Commission Port Moresby, Papua New Guinea, 18 October 1980)

RECOGNIZING EXCESSES

O Ye that are lying as dead on the couch of heedlessness! . . . ye walk on My earth complacent and self-satisfied, heedless that My earth is weary of you and everything within it shunneth you. Were ye but to open your eyes, ye would, in truth, prefer a myriad griefs unto this joy, and would count death itself better than this life. (Bahá'u'lláh, The Hidden Words, Persian, no. 20)

Take from this world only to the measure of your needs and forego that which exceedeth them. Observe equity in all your judgements, and transgress not the bounds of justice, nor be of them that stray from its path. (Bahá'u'lláh, "Súriy-i-Mulúk," *The Summons of the Lord of Hosts*, no. 5.19)

The civilization, so often vaunted by the learned exponents of arts and sciences, will, if allowed to overleap the bounds of moderation, bring great evil upon men. . . . If carried to excess, civilization will prove as prolific a source of evil as it had been of goodness when kept within the restraints of moderation. . . . The day is approaching when its flame will devour the cities. (Bahá'u'lláh *Gleanings from the Writings of Bahá'u'lláh*, no. 164.2)

In all matters moderation is desirable. If a thing is carried to excess, it will prove a source of evil . . . strange and astonishing things exist in the earth but they are hidden from the minds and the understanding of men. These things are capable of changing the whole atmosphere of the earth and their contamination would prove lethal. (Bahá'u'lláh, *Tablets of Bahá'u'lláh*, pp. 68–69)

And the breeding ground of all these tragedies is prejudice: prejudice of race and nation, of religion, of political opinion; and the root

cause of prejudice is blind imitation of the past—imitation in religion, in racial attitudes, in national bias, in politics. So long as this
aping of the past persisteth, just so long will the foundations of the
social order be blown to the four winds, just so long will humanity
be continually exposed to direst peril. ('Abdu'l-Bahá, *Selections from
the Writings of 'Abdu'l-Bahá*, no. 202.3)

Consequently, when thou lookest at the orderly pattern of kingdoms, cities and villages, with the attractiveness of their adornments,
the freshness of their natural resources, the refinement of their appliances, the ease of their means of travel, the extent of knowledge
available about the world of nature, the great inventions, the colossal enterprises, the noble discoveries and scientific researches, thou
wouldst conclude that civilization conduceth to the happiness and
the progress of the human world. Yet shouldst thou turn thine eye to
the discovery of destructive and infernal machines, to the development of forces of demolition and the invention of fiery implements,
which uproot the tree of life, it would become evident and manifest
unto thee that civilization is conjoined with barbarism. Progress and
barbarism go hand in hand, unless material civilization be confirmed
by Divine Guidance, by the revelations of the All-Merciful and by
godly virtues, and be reinforced by spiritual conduct, by the ideals of
the Kingdom and by the outpourings of the Realm of Might.

Consider now, that the most advanced and civilized countries of the
world have been turned into arsenals of explosives, that the continents
of the globe have been transformed into huge camps and battlefields,
that the peoples of the world have formed themselves into armed nations, and that the governments of the world are vying with each other
as to who will first step into the field of carnage and bloodshed, thus
subjecting mankind to the utmost degree of affliction. ('Abdu'l-Bahá,
Selections from the Writings of 'Abdu'l-Bahá, no. 225.5–6)

How terrible it is that men, who are of the higher kingdom, can descend to slaying and bringing misery to their fellow-beings, for the possession of a tract of land! The highest of created beings fighting to obtain the lowest form of matter, earth! Land belongs not to one people, but to all people. This earth is not man's home, but his tomb. It is for their tombs these men are fighting. ('Abdu'l-Bahá, *Paris Talks,* no. 6.1)

We see amongst us men who are overburdened with riches on the one hand, and on the other those unfortunate ones who starve with nothing; those who possess several stately palaces, and those who have not where to lay their head. Some we find with numerous courses of costly and dainty food; whilst others can scarce find sufficient crusts to keep them alive. Whilst some are clothed in velvets, furs and fine linen, others have insufficient, poor and thin garments with which to protect them from the cold. This condition of affairs is wrong, and must be remedied. Now the remedy must be carefully undertaken. It cannot be done by bringing to pass absolute equality between men. ('Abdu'l-Bahá, *Paris Talks,* no. 46.4)

It is quite otherwise with the human race, where the greatest oppression and injustice are to be found. Thus you can observe, on the one hand, a single person who has amassed a fortune, made an entire country his personal dominion, acquired immense wealth, and secured an unceasing flow of gains and profits, and, on the other, a hundred thousand helpless souls—weak, powerless, and wanting even a mouthful of bread. There is neither equality here nor benevolence. Observe how, as a result, general peace and happiness have become so wanting, and the welfare of humanity so undermined, that the lives of a vast multitude have been rendered fruitless! For all the wealth, power, commerce, and industry are concentrated in the hands of a few individuals, while all others toil under the burden of endless hardships and difficulties, are bereft of advantages and benefits, and remain deprived of comfort and peace. ('Abdu'l-Bahá, *Some Answered Questions*, no. 78.4)

Banning nuclear weapons, prohibiting the use of poison gases, or outlawing germ warfare will not remove the root causes of war. However important such practical measures obviously are as elements of the peace process, they are in themselves too superficial to exert enduring influence. Peoples are ingenious enough to invent yet other forms of warfare, and to use, raw materials, finance, industrial power, ideology, and terrorism to subvert one another in an endless quest for supremacy and dominion. Nor can the present massive dislocation in the affairs of humanity be resolved through the settlement of specific conflicts or disagreements among nations. A genuine universal framework must be adopted. (The Universal House of Justice, *The Promise of World Peace*, 1985, To the Peoples of the World)

The time has come when those who preach the dogmas of materialism, whether of the east or of the west, whether of capitalism or socialism, must give account of the moral stewardship they have presumed to exercise. Where is the "new world" promised by these ideologies? . . . Why is the vast majority of the world's peoples sinking ever deeper into hunger and wretchedness when wealth on a scale undreamed of by the Pharaohs, the Caesars, or even the imperialist powers of the nineteenth century is at the disposal of the present arbiters of human affairs? (The Universal House of Justice, *The Promise of World Peace*, 1985, To the Peoples of the World)

The deepening environmental crisis. driven by a system that condones the pillage of natural resources to satisfy an insatiable thirst for more, suggests how entirely inadequate is the present conception of humanity's relationship with nature; the deterioration of the home environment, with the accompanying rise in the systematic exploitation of women and children worldwide, makes clear how pervasive are the misbegotten notions that define relations within the family unit; the persistence of despotism, on the one hand, and the increasing disregard for authority, on the other, reveal how unsatisfactory to a maturing humanity is the current relationship between the individual and the institutions of society; the concentration of material wealth in the hands of a minority of the world's population gives an indication of how fundamentally ill-conceived are relationships among the many sectors of what is now an emerging global community. The principle of the oneness of humankind implies, then, an organic change in the very structure of society. (The Universal House of Justice, message dated 2 March 2013, to the Bahá'ís of Iran)

. . . the end does not serve to justify the means. However constructive and noble the goal, however significant to one's life or to the welfare of one's family, it must not be attained through improper means. Regrettably, a number of today's leaders—political, social, and religious—as well as some of the directors of financial markets, executives of multinational corporations, chiefs of commerce and industry, and ordinary people who succumb to social pressure and ignore the call of their conscience, act against this principle; they justify any means in order to achieve their goals. (The Universal House of Justice, message dated 2 April 2010, to Bahá'ís in the Cradle of the Faith)

The extremes of wealth and poverty in the world are becoming ever more untenable. As inequity persists, so the established order is seen to be unsure of itself, and its values are being questioned. (The Universal House of Justice, message dated 1 March 2017, to the Bahá'ís of the World)

One of the most pressing challenges afflicting multitudes of people across the globe is the disturbed economic situation. The lack of a necessary framework to ensure equity and justice in the distribution of wealth has led to an increase in unemployment and poverty to the extent that even providing life's basic essentials has become extremely difficult for many strata of society. The consequences of the vast divide between the rich and the poor, whether within or among the nations, are indescribable. (The Universal House of Justice, message dated 24 October 2018, to the Bahá'ís of Iran)

The welfare of any segment of humanity is inextricably bound up with the welfare of the whole. Humanity's collective life suffers when any one group thinks of its own well-being in isolation from that of its neighbours or pursues economic gain without regard for how the natural environment, which provides sustenance for all, is affected. A stubborn obstruction, then, stands in the way of meaningful social progress: time and again, avarice and self-interest prevail at the expense of the common good. Unconscionable quantities of wealth are being amassed, and the instability this creates is made worse by how income and opportunity are spread so unevenly both between nations and within nations. But it need not be so. However much such conditions are the outcome of history, they do not have to define the future, and even if current approaches to economic life satisfied humanity's stage of adolescence, they are certainly inadequate for its dawning age of maturity. There is no justification for continuing to perpetuate structures, rules, and systems that manifestly fail to serve the interests of all peoples. The teachings of the Faith leave no room for doubt: there is an inherent moral dimension to the generation, distribution, and utilization of wealth and resources. (The Universal House of Justice, message dated 1 March 2017, to the Bahá'ís of the World)

Racial and ethnic prejudices have been subjected to equally summary treatment by historical processes that have little patience left for such pretensions. Here, rejection of the past has been especially decisive. Racism is now tainted by its association with the horrors of the twentieth century to the degree that it has taken on something of the character of a spiritual disease. While surviving as a social attitude in many parts of the world—and as a blight on the lives of a significant segment of humankind—racial prejudice has become so universally condemned in principle that no body of people can any longer safely allow themselves to be identified with it.

It is not that a dark past has been erased and a new world of light has suddenly been born. Vast numbers of people continue to endure the effects of ingrained prejudices of ethnicity, gender, nation, caste and class. All the evidence indicates that such injustices will long persist as the institutions and standards that humanity is devising only slowly become empowered to construct a new order of relationships and to bring relief to the oppressed. The point, rather, is that a threshold has been crossed from which there is no credible possibility of return. Fundamental principles have been identified, articulated, accorded broad publicity and are becoming progressively incarnated in institutions capable of imposing them on public behaviour. There is no doubt that, however protracted and painful the struggle, the outcome will be to revolutionize relationships among all peoples, at the grassroots level. (The Universal House of Justice, message dated April 2002, to the World's Religious Leaders)

Tragically, organized religion, whose very reason for being entails service to the cause of brotherhood and peace, behaves all too frequently as one of the most formidable obstacles in the path; to cite a particular painful fact, it has long lent its credibility to fanaticism. We feel a responsibility, as the governing council of one of the world religions, to urge earnest consideration of the challenge this poses for religious leadership. (The Universal House of Justice, message dated April 2002, to the World's Religious Leaders)

. . . the letter of the House of Justice dated 1 March 2017, for example, addresses moral questions of consumption and excessive materialism that are associated with the exploitation and degradation of the environment. . . . A moderate perspective is a practical and principled standpoint from which one can recognize and adopt valid and insightful ideas whatever their source, without prejudice. "Whoso cleaveth to justice, can, under no circumstances, transgress the limits of moderation," Bahá'u'lláh states. "He discerneth the truth in all things, through the guidance of Him Who is the All-Seeing." (From a letter written on behalf of the Universal House of Justice, dated 29 November 2017, to three individuals)

By moderation, Bahá'u'lláh is in no way referring to mere compromise, the dilution of truth, or a hypocritical or utopian consensus. The moderation He calls for demands an end to destructive excesses that have plagued humanity and fomented ceaseless contention and turmoil. (From a letter written on behalf of the Universal House of Justice, dated 29 November 2017, to three individuals)

At the same time, Bahá'u'lláh offers a stark warning about the pernicious effects of religious prejudice, stating that "religious fanati-

FOOD, FARMER, AND COMMUNITY

cism and hatred are a world-devouring fire, whose violence none can quench. The Hand of Divine power can, alone, deliver mankind from this desolating affliction." He calls upon Bahá'ís to act so that "the tumult of religious dissension and strife that agitateth the peoples of the earth may be stilled, that every trace of it may be completely obliterated." (From a letter written on behalf of the Universal House of Justice, dated 27 December 2017, to an individual)

The purpose of true religion, then, is to produce good fruits, and if, in the name of religion, conflict, prejudice, and hatred are engendered among humanity, this is due to fallible human interpretations and impositions that can be overcome by seeking the divine truth that lies at the heart of every religion. "May fanaticism and religious bigotry be unknown," He urges, "all humanity enter the bond of brotherhood, souls consort in perfect agreement, the nations of earth at last hoist the banner of truth, and the religions of the world enter the divine temple of oneness, for the foundations of the heavenly religions are one reality." (From a letter written on behalf of the Universal House of Justice, dated 27 December 2017, to an individual)

. . . it is the concentration of wealth in the hands of the few that is in urgent need of attention. Indeed, the tremendous wealth generated by transnational corporations could be an integral part of the solution to tackle poverty, through strict regulation to ensure good global citizenship, adherence to human rights norms and the distribution of wealth for the benefit of the larger society. (Bahá'í International Community, "Eradicating Poverty: Moving Forward as One," the Bahá'í International Community's Statement on Poverty, 14 February 2008)

A challenge of similar nature faces economic thinking as a result of the environmental crisis. The fallacies in theories based on the belief that there is no limit to nature's capacity to fulfil any demand made on it by human beings have now been coldly exposed. A culture which attaches absolute value to expansion, to acquisition, and to the satisfaction of people's wants is being compelled to recognise that such goals are not, by themselves, realistic guides to policy. Inadequate, too, are approaches to economic issues whose decision-making tools cannot deal with the fact that most of the major challenges are global rather than particular in scope. *(The Prosperity of Humankind.* A statement prepared by the Bahá'í International Community Office of Public Information, Haifa, 1995)

Against the backdrop of climate change, environmental degradation, and the crippling extremes of wealth and poverty, the transformation from a culture of unfettered consumerism to a culture of sustainability has gained momentum in large part through the efforts of civil society organizations and governmental agencies worldwide. . . . The issue of sustainable consumption and production . . . will need to be considered in the broader context of an ailing social order—one characterized by competition, violence, conflict and insecurity—of which it is a part. (Bahá'í International Community, "Rethinking Prosperity: Forging Alternatives to a Culture of Consumerism," 2010)

The unrestrained exploitation of natural resources is merely a symptom of an overall sickness of the human spirit. Any solutions to the environment/development crisis must, therefore, be rooted in an approach which fosters spiritual balance and harmony within the individual, between individuals, and with the environment as a whole.

Material development must serve not only the body, but the mind and spirit as well. (Bahá'í International Community, "Earth Charter, 5 April 1991." The following statement offering suggestions for the proposed "Earth Charter," was originally presented by the Bahá'í International Community to the Preparatory Committee of the United Nations Conference on Environment and Development (UNCED), June 1992)

The rapid progress in science and technology that has united the world physically has also greatly accelerated destruction of the biological diversity and rich natural heritage with which the planet has been endowed. Material civilization, driven by the dogmas of consumerism and aggressive individualism and disoriented by the weakening of moral standards and spiritual values, has been carried to excess. Only a comprehensive vision of a global society, supported by universal values and principles, can inspire individuals to take responsibility for the long-term care and protection of the natural environment. (Bahá'í International Community, "Conservation and Sustainable Development in the Bahá'í Faith." This paper was presented by the Bahá'í International Community to the Summit on the Alliance Between Religions and Conservation, 3 May 1995)

It has been widely acknowledged that economic prosperity has come at a tremendous cost to our natural environment. In fact, no country has emerged as a major industrial power without a legacy of significant environmental damage, affecting the security and well-being of its own populations and, equally significantly, those of developing nations. The growth-driven economic paradigm rooted in national interests at the expense of social and environmental variables and international well-being is under increasing scrutiny. (Bahá'í International Community, "Eradicating Poverty: Moving Forward as

One," the Bahá'í International Community's Statement on Poverty, 14 February 2008)

ADDENDUM

DIVINE ASSISTANCE FOR TRYING TIMES

The Bahá'í writings provide a sustaining source of spiritual practices essential in a search for deeper meanings to life's material challenges.

STRIVING FOR SPIRITUAL SUSTENANCE

Success or failure, gain or loss, must, therefore, depend upon man's own exertions. The more he striveth, the greater will be his progress. We fain would hope that the vernal showers of the bounty of God may cause the flowers of true understanding to spring from the soil of men's hearts, and may wash them from all earthly defilements. (Bahá'u'lláh, *Gleanings from the Writings of Bahá'u'lláh*, no. 34.8)

O thou who art turning thy face towards God! Close thine eyes to all things else, and open them to the realm of the All-Glorious. Ask whatsoever thou wishest of Him alone; seek whatsoever thou seekest from Him alone. With a look He granteth a hundred thousand hopes, with a glance He healeth a hundred thousand incurable ills, with a nod He layeth balm on every wound, with a glimpse He freeth the hearts from the shackles of grief. He doeth as He doeth, and what recourse have we? He carrieth out His Will, He ordaineth what He pleaseth. Then better for thee to bow down thy head in submission, and put thy trust in the All-Merciful Lord. ('Abdu'l-Bahá, *Selections from the Writings of 'Abdu'l-Bahá*, no. 22.1)

Commerce, agriculture and industry should not, in truth, be a bar to service of the one true God. Indeed, such occupations are most potent instruments and clear proofs for the manifestation of the evidences of one's piety, of one's trustworthiness and of the virtues of the All-Merciful Lord. ('Abdu'l-Bahá, from a Tablet translated from the Persian, in *Trustworthiness: A Compilation Prepared by the Research Department of the Universal House of Justice*)

TESTS

But inasmuch as the divine Purpose hath decreed that the true should be known from the false, and the sun from the shadow, He hath, therefore, in every season sent down upon mankind the showers of tests from His realm of glory. (Bahá'u'lláh, The Kitáb-i-Íqán, ¶56)

O Son of Man! My calamity is My providence, outwardly it is fire and vengeance, but inwardly it is light and mercy. Hasten thereunto that thou mayest become an eternal light and an immortal spirit. This is My command unto thee, do thou observe it. (Bahá'u'lláh, The Hidden Words, Arabic, no. 51)

O Son of My Handmaid! Be not troubled in poverty nor confident in riches, for poverty is followed by riches, and riches are followed by poverty. (Bahá'u'lláh, The Hidden Words, Persian, no. 51)

O Son of Spirit! Ask not of Me that which We desire not for thee, then be content with what We have ordained for thy sake, for this is that which profiteth thee, if therewith thou dost content thyself. (Bahá'u'lláh, The Hidden Words, Arabic, no. 18)

The beloved of the Lord must stand fixed as the mountains, firm as impregnable walls. Unmoved must they remain by even the direst adversities, ungrieved by the worst of disasters. Let them cling to the hem of Almighty God, and put their faith in the Beauty of the Most High; let them lean on the unfailing help that cometh from the Ancient Kingdom, and depend on the care and protection of the generous Lord. ('Abdu'l-Bahá, *Selections from the Writings of 'Abdu'l-Bahá*, no. 2.15)

Tests are benefits from God, for which we should thank Him. Grief and sorrow do not come to us by chance, they are sent to us by the Divine Mercy for our own perfecting.

While a man is happy he may forget his God; but when grief comes and sorrows overwhelm him, then will he remember his Father who is in Heaven, and who is able to deliver him from his humiliations.

Men who suffer not, attain no perfection. The plant most pruned by the gardeners is that one which, when the summer comes, will have the most beautiful blossoms and the most abundant fruit.

The laborer cuts up the earth with his plough, and from that earth comes the rich and plentiful harvest. The more a man is chastened, the greater is the harvest of spiritual virtues shown forth by him. A soldier is no good General until he has been in the front of the fiercest battle and has received the deepest wounds. ('Abdu'l-Bahá, *Paris Talks*, no. 14.7–10)

In this world we are influenced by two sentiments, Joy and Pain. . . .

There is no human being untouched by these two influences; but all the sorrow and the grief that exist come from the world of matter—the spiritual world bestows only the joy! If we suffer it is the outcome of material things, and all the trials and troubles come from this world of illusion.

For instance, a merchant may lose his trade and depression ensues. A workman is dismissed and starvation stares him in the face. A farmer has a bad harvest, anxiety fills his mind. A man builds a house which is burnt to the ground and he is straightway homeless, ruined, and in despair.

All these examples are to show you that the trials which beset our every step, all our sorrow, pain, shame and grief, are born in the world of matter, whereas the spiritual Kingdom never causes sadness. A man living with his thoughts in this Kingdom knows perpetual joy. The ills all flesh is heir to do not pass him by, but they only touch the surface of his life, the depths are calm and serene. ('Abdu'l-Bahá, *Paris Talks*, no. 35.1–6)

PRAYER

Blessed is the spot, and the house, and the place, and the city, and the heart, and the mountain, and the refuge, and the cave, and the valley, and the land, and the sea, and the island, and the meadow where mention of God hath been made, and His praise glorified. (Bahá'u'lláh, in *Bahá'í Prayers*, p. ii)

At the dawn of every day he should commune with God, and with all his soul persevere in the quest of his Beloved. (Bahá'u'lláh, The Kitáb-i-Íqán, ¶214)

On the appearance of fearful natural events call ye to mind the might and majesty of your Lord, He Who heareth and seeth all, and say "Dominion is God's, the Lord of the seen and the unseen, the Lord of creation." (Bahá'u'lláh, The Kitáb-i-Aqdas, ¶11)

In regard to his affairs, let him repeat nineteen times: "Thou seest me, O my God, detached from all save Thee and cleaving unto

Thee. Guide me, then, in all mine affairs unto that which profiteth me for the glory of Thy Cause and the loftiness of the station of Thy loved ones." Let him then reflect upon the matter and undertake whatever cometh to mind. This vehement opposition of the enemies will indeed give way to supreme prosperity. (Bahá'u'lláh, Additional Prayers Revealed by Bahá'u'lláh, https://www.bahai.org/library/authoritative-texts/bahaullah/)

He is God, exalted is He, the Lord of might and grandeur!
O God, my God! I yield Thee thanks at all times and render Thee praise under all conditions.

In prosperity, all praise is Thine, O Lord of the Worlds, and in its absence, all gratitude is Thine, O Desire of them that have recognized Thee!

In adversity, all honour is Thine, O Adored One of all who are in heaven and on earth, and in affliction, all glory is Thine, O Enchanter of the hearts of those who yearn after Thee!

In hardship, all praise is Thine, O Thou the Goal of them that seek after Thee, and in comfort, all thanksgiving is Thine, O Thou whose remembrance is treasured in the hearts of those who are nigh unto Thee!

In wealth, all splendour is Thine, O Lord of them that are devoted to Thee, and in poverty, all command is Thine, O Thou the Hope of them that acknowledge Thy unity!

In joy, all glory is Thine, O Thou besides Whom there is none other God, and in sorrow, all beauty is Thine, O Thou besides Whom there is none other God!

In hunger, all justice is Thine, O Thou besides Whom there is none other God, and in satiety, all grace is Thine, O Thou besides Whom there is none other God! (Bahá'u'lláh, Additional Prayers

Revealed by Bahá'u'lláh, https://www.bahai.org/library/authoritative-texts/bahaullah/)

... I am, O my God, but a tiny seed which Thou hast sown in the soil of Thy love, and caused to spring forth by the hand of Thy bounty. This seed craveth, therefore, in its inmost being, for the waters of Thy mercy and the living fountain of Thy grace. Send down upon it, from the heaven of Thy loving-kindness, that which will enable it to flourish beneath Thy shadow and within the borders of Thy court. Thou art He Who watereth the hearts of all that have recognized Thee from Thy plenteous stream and the fountain of Thy living waters.

Praised be God, the Lord of the worlds. (Bahá'u'lláh, *Prayers and Meditations*, no. 106.3–4)

Is there any Remover of Difficulties, save God? Say: Praised be God. He is God. All are His servants and all abide by His bidding. (The Báb, *Selections from the Writings of the Báb*, no. 7.48)

Say: God sufficeth all things above all things, and nothing in the heavens or in the earth or in whatever lieth between them but God, thy Lord, sufficeth. Verily, He is in Himself the Knower, the Sustainer, the Omnipotent. (The Báb, *Selections from the Writings of the Báb*, no. 4.8.1)

O my God, O my God! Verily this plant hath yielded its fruit and standeth upright upon its stalk. Verily it hath astounded the farmers and perturbed the envious. O God, water it with showers from the cloud of Thy favours and cause it to yield great harvests heaped up like unto mighty hills in Thy land. Enlighten the hearts with a ray shining forth from Thy Kingdom of Oneness, illumine the eyes by beholding the signs of Thy grace, and gratify the ears by hearing the melodies of the birds of Thy confirmations singing in Thy heavenly gardens, so that these souls may become like thirsty fish swimming in the pools of Thy guidance and like tawny lions roaming in the forests of Thy bounty. Verily Thou art the Generous, the Merciful, the Glorious and the Bestower. ('Abdu'l-Bahá, Additional Prayers Revealed by 'Abdu'l-Bahá, https://www.bahai.org/library/authoritative-texts/abdul-baha/)

O God! Dispel all those elements which are the cause of discord, and prepare for us all those things which are the cause of unity and accord! O God! Descend upon us Heavenly Fragrance and change this gathering into a gathering of Heaven! Grant to us every benefit and every food. Prepare for us the Food of Love! Give us the Food of Knowledge! Bestow on us the Food of Heavenly Illumination! ('Abdu'l-Bahá, in *Star of the West*, vol. 4, no. 7, p. 120)

Therefore strive that your actions day by day may be beautiful prayers. ('Abdu'l-Bahá, *Paris Talks*, no. 26.7)

MEDITATION

Look at the world and ponder a while upon it. It unveileth the book of its own self before thine eyes and revealeth that which the Pen of thy Lord, the Fashioner, the All-Informed, hath inscribed therein. It will acquaint thee with that which is within it and upon it and will give thee such clear explanations as to make thee independent of every eloquent expounder. (Bahá'u'lláh, *Tablets of Bahá'u'lláh*, p. 141)

So long as the thoughts of an individual are scattered he will achieve no results, but if his thinking be concentrated on a single point wonderful will be the fruits thereof.

237

One cannot obtain the full force of the sunlight when it is cast on a flat mirror, but once the sun shineth upon a concave mirror, or on a lens that is convex, all its heat will be concentrated on a single point, and that one point will burn the hottest. Thus is it necessary to focus one's thinking on a single point so that it will become an effective force. ('Abdu'l-Bahá, *Selections from the Writings of 'Abdu'l-Bahá*, no. 73.1–2)

Through the faculty of meditation man attains to eternal life; through it he receives the breath of the Holy Spirit—the bestowal of the Spirit is given in reflection and meditation.

The spirit of man is itself informed and strengthened during meditation; through it affairs of which man knew nothing are unfolded before his view. Through it he receives Divine inspiration, through it he receives heavenly food.

Meditation is the key for opening the doors of mysteries. In that state man abstracts himself: in that state man withdraws himself from all outside objects; in that subjective mood he is immersed in the ocean of spiritual life and can unfold the secrets of things-in-themselves. To illustrate this, think of man as endowed with two kinds of sight; when the power of insight is being used the outward power of vision does not see.

This faculty of meditation frees man from the animal nature, discerns the reality of things, puts man in touch with God.

This faculty brings forth from the invisible plane the sciences and arts. Through the meditative faculty inventions are made possible, colossal undertakings are carried out; through it governments can run smoothly. Through this faculty man enters into the very Kingdom of God. ('Abdu'l-Bahá, *Paris Talks,* no. 54.11–15)

O Lord, help Thou Thy loved ones to acquire knowledge and the sciences and arts, and to unravel the secrets that are treasured up in the inmost reality of all created beings. Make them to hear the hidden truths that are written and embedded in the heart of all that is. Make them to be ensigns of guidance amongst all creatures, and piercing rays of the mind shedding forth their light in this, the "first life." Make them to be leaders unto Thee, guides unto Thy path, runners urging men on to Thy Kingdom. Thou verily art the Powerful, the Protector, the Potent, the Defender, the Mighty, the Most Generous. ('Abdu'l-Bahá, in *Bahá'í Prayers*, p. 115)

If you read the utterances of Bahá'u'lláh and 'Abdu'l-Bahá with selflessness and care and concentrate upon them, you will discover truths unknown to you before and will obtain an insight into the problems that have baffled the great thinkers of the world. (Shoghi Effendi, handwritten note appended to a letter dated 30 January 1925, written on behalf of Shoghi Effendi to an individual believer, in *Living the Life*, p. 4)

In His talks 'Abdu'l-Bahá describes prayer as "conversation with God," and concerning meditation He says that "while you meditate you are speaking with your own spirit. In that state of mind you put certain questions to your spirit and the spirit answers: the light breaks forth and the reality is revealed." (The Universal House of Justice, letter dated 1 September 1983, to the National Spiritual Assembly of the Bahá'ís of Norway)

FASTING

Fasting and obligatory prayer constitute the two pillars that sustain the revealed Law of God. Bahá'u'lláh in one of His Tablets affirms that He has revealed the laws of obligatory prayer and fasting so that through them the believers may draw nigh unto God. Shoghi Effendi indicates that the fasting period, which involves complete abstention from food and drink from sunrise till sunset, is essentially a period of meditation and prayer, of spiritual recuperation, during which the believer must strive to make the necessary readjustments in his inner life, and to refresh and reinvigorate the spiritual forces latent in his soul. Its significance and purpose are, therefore, fundamentally spiritual in character. Fasting is symbolic, and a reminder of abstinence from selfish and carnal desires. Fasting is enjoined on all the believers once they attain the age of 15 and until they reach the age of 70 years. (Universal House of Justice, *The Kitáb-i-Aqdas*, Notes, no. 25)

Exemption from fasting is granted to those who are ill or of advanced age . . . women in their courses, travelers . . . and to women who are pregnant and those who are nursing. This exemption is also extended to people who are engaged in heavy labor, who, at the same time, are advised "to show respect to the law of God and for the exalted station of the Fast" by eating "with frugality and in private . . ." (Universal House of Justice, *The Kitáb-i-Aqdas*, Notes, no. 31)

THE PROMISE

O Son of Man! Thou art My dominion and My dominion perisheth not, wherefore fearest thou thy perishing? Thou art My light and My light shall never be extinguished, why dost thou dread extinction? Thou art My glory and My glory fadeth not; thou art My robe and My robe shall never be outworn. Abide then in thy love for Me, that thou mayest find Me in the realm of glory. (Bahá'u'lláh, The Hidden Words, Arabic, no. 14)

The time foreordained unto the peoples and kindreds of the earth is now come. The promises of God, as recorded in the holy Scriptures, have all been fulfilled. Out of Zion hath gone forth the Law of God, and Jerusalem, and the hills and land thereof, are filled with the glory of His Revelation. Happy is the man that pondereth in his heart that which hath been revealed in the Books of God, the Help in Peril, the Self-Subsisting. Meditate upon this, O ye beloved of God, and let your ears be attentive unto His Word, so that ye may, by His grace and mercy, drink your fill from the crystal waters of constancy, and become as steadfast and immovable as the mountain in His Cause. (Bahá'u'lláh, *Gleanings from the Writings of Bahá'u'lláh*, no. 10.1)

Such simultaneous processes of rise and of fall, of integration and of disintegration, of order and chaos, with their continuous and reciprocal reactions on each other, are but aspects of a greater Plan, one and indivisible, whose Source is God, whose author is Bahá'u'lláh, the theater of whose operations is the entire planet, and whose ultimate objectives are the unity of the human race and the peace of all mankind. (Shoghi Effendi, *Advent of Divine Justice*, ¶103)

The world is, in truth, moving on towards its destiny. The interdependence of the peoples and nations of the earth, whatever the leaders of the divisive forces of the world may say or do, is already an accomplished fact. Its unity in the economic sphere is now understood and recognized. The welfare of the part means the welfare of the whole, and the distress of the part brings distress to the whole. The Revelation of Bahá'u'lláh has, in His own words, "lent a fresh impulse and set a new direction" to this vast process now operating in the world. The fires lit by this great ordeal are the consequences of men's failure to recognize it. They are, moreover, hastening its consummation. Adversity, prolonged, worldwide, afflictive, allied to chaos and universal destruction, must needs convulse the nations, stir the conscience of the world, disillusion the masses, precipitate a radical change in the very conception of society, and coalesce ultimately the disjointed, the bleeding limbs of mankind into one body, single, organically united, and indivisible. (Shoghi Effendi, *The Promised Day Is Come*, ¶300)

. . . we cite the emphatic promise of Bahá'u'lláh: "These fruitless strifes, these ruinous wars shall pass away, and the 'Most Great Peace' shall come. " (The Universal House of Justice, *The Promise of World Peace*, 1985, To the Peoples of the World)

For Bahá'ís, Bahá'u'lláh's promise that civilization will exist on this planet for a minimum of five thousand centuries makes it unconscionable to ignore the long-term impact of decisions made today. . . . the world civilization that Bahá'ís believe will eventually emerge will be animated by a deep religious faith and will be one in which science and technology will serve humanity and help it to live in harmony with nature. (Bahá'í International Community, "Conservation and Sustainable Development in the Bahá'í Faith," paper presented by the Bahá'í International Community to the Summit on the Alliance Between Religions and Conservation, 3 May 1995)

BIBLIOGRAPHY

Works of Bahá'u'lláh

Epistle to the Son of the Wolf. 1st pocket-size ed. Translated by Shoghi Effendi. Wilmette, IL: Bahá'í Publishing Trust, 1988.

Gleanings from the Writings of Bahá'u'lláh. Translated by Shoghi Effendi. Wilmette, IL: Bahá'í Publishing, 2005.

The Hidden Words. Translated by Shoghi Effendi. Wilmette, IL: Bahá'í Publishing, 2002.

The Kitáb-i-Aqdas: The Most Holy Book. 1st pocket-size ed. Wilmette, IL: Bahá'í Publishing Trust, 1993.

The Kitáb-i-Íqán: The Book of Certitude. Translated by Shoghi Effendi. Wilmette, IL: Bahá'í Publishing, 2003.

Prayers and Meditations. Translated by Shoghi Effendi. 1st pocket-size ed. Wilmette, IL: Bahá'í Publishing Trust, 1987.

The Summons of the Lord of Hosts: Tablets of Bahá'u'lláh. Wilmette: Bahá'í Publishing, 2006.

The Tabernacle of Unity: Bahá'u'lláh's Responses to Mánikchí Sáhib and Other Writings. Haifa: Bahá'í World Centre, 2006.

Tablets of Bahá'u'lláh revealed after the Kitáb-i-Aqdas. Compiled by the Research Department of the Universal House of Justice. Translated by Habib Taherzadeh et al. Wilmette, IL: 1988.

Works of the Báb

Selections from the Writings of the Báb. Translated by Habib Taherzadeh and a committee at the Bahá'í World Center. Wilmette: Bahá'í Publishing, 2005.

Works of 'Abdu'l-Bahá

'Abdu'l-Bahá in London: Addresses and Notes of Conversations. London: Bahá'í Publishing Trust, 1982.

Memorials of the Faithful. Translated by Marzieh Gail. Wilmette, IL: Bahá'í Publishing Trust, 1997.

Paris Talks: Addresses Given By 'Abdu'l-Bahá in Paris in 1911. 12th ed. London: Bahá'í Publishing, 2011.

Pearls of Bounty: Selections from the Prayers, Tablets, and Talks of 'Abdu'l-Bahá. Wilmette, IL: Bahá'í Publishing, 2021

The Promulgation of Universal Peace: Talks Delivered by 'Abdu'l-Bahá during His Visit to the United States and Canada in 1912. Compiled by Howard MacNutt. 2d ed. Wilmette, IL: Bahá'í Publishing, 2012.

Selections from the Writings of 'Abdu'l-Bahá. Compiled by the Research Department of the Universal House of Justice. Translated by a Committee at the Bahá'í World Center and Marzieh Gail. Wilmette, IL: Bahá'í Publishing, 2010.

Some Answered Questions. Haifa: Bahá'í World Centre, 2014.

Works of Shoghi Effendi

Advent of Divine Justice. 1st pocket-size ed. Wilmette, IL: Bahá'í Publishing Trust, 1990.

Bahá'í Administration: Selected Messages 1922–1932. 7th ed. Wilmette, IL: Bahá'í Publishing Trust, 1974.

Directives from the Guardian. Wilmette, IL: Bahá'í Publishing Trust, 1973.

God Passes By. New ed. Wilmette, IL: Bahá'í Publishing Trust, 1974.

The Promised Day Is Come. 1st pocket-size ed. Wilmette, IL: Bahá'í Publishing Trust, 1996.

The World Order of Bahá'u'lláh: Selected Letters. 1st pocket-size ed. Wilmette, IL: Bahá'í Publishing Trust, 1991.

Works of the Universal House of Justice

Messages from the Universal House of Justice, 1963–1986: The Third Epoch of the Formative Age. Compiled by Geoffry Marks. Wilmette, IL: Bahá'í Publishing Trust, 1996.

Messages from the Universal House of Justice, 1968–1973. Haifa: Bahá'í World Center, 1973.

Messages from the Universal House of Justice, 1986–2001: The Fourth Epoch of the Formative Age. Compiled by Geoffry Marks. Wilmette, IL: Bahá'í Publishing Trust, 2010.

The Promise of World Peace: To the Peoples of the World. Wilmette, IL: Bahá'í Publishing Trust, 1985.

A Wider Horizon, Selected Letters 1983–1992. West Palm Beach, FL: Palabra Publications, 1992.

Compilations of Bahá'í Writings

Agriculture and Rural Life. A compilation prepared by the Research Department of the Universal House of Justice. Haifa: Bahá'í World Center, 1995.

Bahá'í Prayers: A Selection of Prayers Revealed by Bahá'u'lláh, the Báb, and 'Abdu'l-Bahá. New ed. Wilmette, IL: Bahá'í Publishing Trust, 2002.

The Compilation of Compilations: Prepared by the Universal House of Justice, 1963–1990. 3 vols. Australia: Bahá'í Publications Australia, 1991.

"Economics, Agriculture, and Related Subjects," in *The Compilation of Compilations,* vol. 3. Australia: Bahá'í Publications Australia, 2000.

Ḥuqúqu'lláh—The Right of God: A Compilation of Extracts from the Writings of Bahá'u'lláh and 'Abdu'l-Bahá and from Letters Written by and on behalf of Shoghi Effendi and the Universal House of Justice. Wilmette, IL: Bahá'í Publishing Trust, 2009.

The Institution of the Mashriqu'l-Adhkár. A Statement Prepared by the Research Department of the Universal House of Justice, September 2017.

Lights of Guidance: A Bahá'í Reference File. Compiled by Helen Hornby. New ed. New Dehli, India: Bahá'í Publishing Trust, 1994.

Prayer and Devotional Life. A compilation prepared by the Research Department of the Universal House of Justice. Wilmette, IL: Bahá'í Publishing, 2019.

"Reproduction and other Biological Subjects." A Compilation Prepared by the Research Department of the Universal House of Justice. Haifa: Bahá'í World Center, 2000.

"Trustworthiness." A compilation prepared by the Research Department of the Universal House of Justice. Haifa: Bahá'í World Center, 1990.

Statements of the Bahá'í International Community

"Advocates for African Food Security: Lessening the Burden for Women, Joint statement to the 35th session of the United Nations Commission on the Status of Women," 27 February 1991

"Bahá'í International Community's Plan of Action on Climate Change," 2009.

"The Bahá'í Statement on Nature," 1987.

"Conservation and Sustainable Development in the Bahá'í Faith," paper presented by the Bahá'í International Community to the Summit on the Alliance Between Religions and Conservation, 3 May 1995.

"Contribution to the 56th Session of the United Nations Commission on the Status of Women," New York, 27 February 2012.

"Earth Charter," 5 April 1991. Statement offering suggestions for the proposed "Earth Charter," originally presented by the Bahá'í International Community to the Preparatory Committee of the United Nations Conference on Environment and Development (UNCED), June 1992.

"The Earth Charter/Rio De Janeiro Declaration and the Oneness of Humanity," UN, 1997.

"Eradicating Poverty: Moving Forward as One." The Bahá'í International Community's Statement on Poverty, 14 February 2008.

"Moral and Ethical Dimensions of Climate Change: Appeal to the World's Leaders," September 2009

"The Prosperity of Humankind." A statement prepared by the Bahá'í International Community Office of Public Information, Haifa, first distributed at the United Nations World Summit on Social Development, Copenhagen, Denmark, 3 March 1995.

"Rethinking Prosperity: Forging Alternatives to a Culture of Consumerism," Bahá'í International Community's Contribution to the 18th Session of the United Nations Commission on Sustainable Development, 3 May 2010.

"Seizing the Opportunity: Redefining the challenge of climate change, Initial Considerations of the Bahá'í International Community," 1 December 2008.

"Shared Vision, Shared Volition: Choosing Our Global Future Together," a statement of the Bahá'í International Community to the United Nations Climate Change Conference in Paris, France, 23 November 2015.

"Spiritual and Social Values for Rural Development," paper presented to the Twentieth Conference of the South Pacific Commission Port Moresby, Papua New Guinea, 18 October 1980.

"Statement on Sustainable Communities in an Integrating World," 1996.

"Toward a New Discourse on Religion and Gender Equality," 1 February 2015.

"Valuing Spirituality in Development: Initial Considerations Regarding the Creation of Spiritually Based Indicators for Development." A concept paper written for the World Faiths and Development Dialogue, Lambeth Palace, London, 18–19 February 1998.

"Who is Writing the Future," 1999.

Other Works

The Bahá'í World: A Biennial International Record, Vol. IV. Haifa, Israel: The Universal House of Justice, 1932.

"Social Action." A paper prepared by the Office of Social and Economic Development at the Bahá'í World Center, 26 November 2012.

Star of the West. Multiple volumes cited.